DUCK HUNTING

OTHER BOOKS IN THE SPORTSMAN'S LIBRARY

By William F. Brown:

FIELD TRIALS

HOW TO TRAIN HUNTING DOGS

RETRIEVER GUN DOGS

By E. C. Janes:

A BOY AND HIS GUN

By Bert Popowski:

CROW SHOOTING

By Dick Shaughnessy with Tap Goodenough:

SKEET AND TRAPSHOOTING

By J. Edson Leonard:

FLIES

By H. G. Tapply:

TACKLE TINKERING

FIGURE 1 *Black ducks and mallards.*

DUCK HUNTING

by John G. MacKenty

A. S. Barnes and Company

New York

PUBLISHED ON THE SAME DAY IN THE DOMINION OF CANADA
BY THE COPP CLARK COMPANY, LTD., TORONTO.

LIBRARY OF CONGRESS CATALOG CARD NUMBER: 53-8302

To DOROTHY M. FLYNN

ACKNOWLEDGMENTS

I gratefully acknowledge the many criticisms of and helpful suggestions on this book, so generously contributed by my friends and fellow gunners, Miss Dorothy M. Flynn, Mrs. Peter Geddes, Mrs. Morgan K. Smith, Jr., R. H. Bayard Bowie, Richard L. Colter, Rogers C. Doering, Harry Durand, Charles Medeiros, my son-in-law, Robert P. Bigelow, and my son, John E. MacKenty. Without their assistance the following pages would include more imperfections than they now contain.

So, I express appreciation to them and to the following of my friends, who did not have to suffer with the manuscript, but with whom I have spent, over the past years, many, many happy hours learning at first hand the few facets of the complex but always absorbing art of Duck Hunting which are set forth in these pages: Ewen C. Anderson, C. Stuart Avery, George H. Carey, Richard I. Colter, Peter Geddes, Landon Humphreys, Malcolm Keniston, Morgan K. Smith, Jr., Dr. Charles A. Sprague, Edward L. Stevenson, and my daughter, Mrs. Robert P. Bigelow.

Lastly, I want to thank Miss Martha E. Smith and Mrs. Josephine R. Walker who typed and retyped the manuscript so many times.

FIGURE 2 *Hen black ducks and mallard drakes.*

INTRODUCTION

It is with a mixed feeling of humility and inadequacy that I approach the task of writing the ensuing pages of this little book.

The feeling of humility arises from the recognition of my good fortune in having been able to do a good deal of duck hunting, particularly in the past ten years, and that of inadequacy comes from the realization that if one were accorded the life span of Methuselah, a permanent open season and the wherewithal to go hunting every day, one would still not be an absolute expert in this infinitely varied and always absorbing sport.

In the absence of these advantages, this book attempts to set forth only the few scattered scraps of experience and knowledge gathered over many years of duck hunting—or gunning, as we term it here in New England.

That leads me to make an admission, here at the beginning, that my duck hunting has been confined to the northeastern part of the United States. Thus it may be that a few parts of some of the chapters may not be entirely applicable to the Mississippi flyway and to the Pacific States; and some of the methods used in those sections may have been omitted from these pages. Most of this book, however, applies to duck hunting anywhere. Therefore, this is the point at which you fellows, who live west of the Appalachians and who have read this far in the Introduction, can take this volume back to your book dealer for credit before it gets dog-eared or spattered with tears of disappointment.

This book is directed at the man who makes all his own preparations for duck hunting—building his own blinds, stringing his own decoys and assuming all the comparatively onerous accompanying functions of setting them out and picking them up while a flock of twenty scaup try to knock his cap off, dragging and rowing heavy boats and chasing and disposing of cripples. To the man who does not do these things for himself, this book—if he reads it—may merely point out that there is more to duck hunting than pulling the trigger.

JOHN G. MACKENTY
EDGARTOWN
MASSACHUSETTS
1953

CONTENTS

DUCK HUNTING

chapter one

WHY DO WE GO DUCK HUNTING?

The basic answer to this question would lie in a well-stirred combination of philosophy and psychology, so we shall deal but briefly with this aspect before we pass on to the other reasons.

It is atavistic to want to hunt something, be it deer, or upland birds or squirrels or even fish. Deeply ingrained, in whatever parts of our beings represent a distillation of the characters of our ancestors, is the desire to hunt—to bring back meat to the little woman and the childer huddled over the smoking fire at the back of the cave. Furthermore—to appease those who deny the inheritance of acquired characteristics—most Americans have heard, ever since they were tall enough to rest their chins on grandfather's knee, that hunting was a noble and commendable occupation, sometimes frowned upon by the distaff side of the family because of its interference with the performance of household chores, but rendered thereby all the more popular due to its promotion of that superficial conflict which almost always exists between the sexes.

Overlying this basic urge to hunt are a thousand and one reasons why hunting—particularly duck hunting—is a desirable and delightful occupation, Cornelia Otis Skinner to the contrary notwithstanding.

I would like to digress here for a moment and point out that I employ the term "duck hunting" throughout this volume instead of the expression "duck shooting." This is done first in the cause of accuracy, for surely, one does not always shoot when one hunts. Secondly, ninety per cent of the pleasure in this sport lies in the process of *hunting* and perhaps only ten per cent in the actual "shooting." One would not want to call it "duck killing." That would contain all the implied charms and attractions of an abattoir.

Well, back to the other reasons for duck hunting.

First, perhaps, it offers such an extreme contrast to whatever it is we do to earn our respective livings and thus make it possible for us to go duck hunting.

Duck hunting is conducted in a pleasurable and paradoxical atmosphere of relaxation and anticipatory tension. You never know what is going to happen next—but something usually does.

The companionship, the joint and co-operative effort of two or three men stalking a pothole or huddled in a blind or rowing a stubborn boat among the ice cakes after a cripple, seems to engender a relationship that the conflicts and vicissitudes of everyday life cannot impair.

Perhaps chief to me among the collateral reasons is the complete opportunity to be one with nature at the time of its most charming and delightful mood—dawn.

You get up in the cold dark and attempt, probably unsuccessfully, to appraise the weather through the reflecting glass of the window, which casts back principally an underexposed photograph of the familiar objects in your room. Wisely you decide to don the extra heavy underwear anyway.

Now, if you had to get up at this God-awful hour to catch a train, or as I do, take an early boat to the mainland, you would probably be half drowned in your own tears of self-pity; but these circumstances are, of course, entirely different. If someone in the house is going hunting with you, the joint breakfast will be as gay as a wedding. Even if you breakfast alone, the prospect of the hours ahead brightens what would otherwise be a lugubrious meal.

The group with whom I hunt usually meet at my house for prehunting coffee; but, inasmuch as all of them have had coffee before they arrived, this is really mostly an excuse to review the incidents and accidents of the previous day, and to kid the perpetrator of the latest damn fool mistake made in boat or blind the day before. Pontifical statements are delivered about the wind, the temperature, the possibility of rain or snow, the number of ducks seen where yesterday; and rash and positive conclusions–which usually fail to be borne out–are made as to the effect of all of these upon the success of the day which is about to dawn.

Now, boots are grunted on, gunning coats are struggled into, cartridge belts are strapped on, and guns and gunning bags are loaded into the cars waiting outside–for this year I have four blinds on my place and there are eight of us occupying them. Someone who scorns cartridge belts drops a box of shells and, booted and bundled up as we are, we groaningly retrieve the shells from under chairs, tables and couches. I have never believed that the flimsy box in which manufacturers pack shells is a suitable container to be carried into a blind.

After I have scraped the eighth inch of frost off my windshield, the four cars start out in single file, lights bobbing over the rough surfaces of what I euphemistically term roads. Through the chill misty air of late autumn, through pasture and forest we crawl along–down toward the shore.

There is a very special magic about the hour before dawn. Places utterly familiar in daylight assume a mystical and unfamiliar aspect. The boles of the trees slide by like ghosts at the side where the headlights do not strike them directly. The points of frost on the grass blade and sleeping blueberry bush twinkle a reflected light back to us as if they were a myriad frozen fireflies.

This morning it is still. There is no wind at all and hence the heavy frost. A sliver of a new moon is setting in the west and it keeps pace with us, skipping through the bare branches of the oaks or hiding behind a pine only to pop out again and resume its apparent parallel motion.

One by one the cars peel off on side lanes to their assigned blinds, and we continue alone to ours.

It is still dark, as it should be at the time of arrival at a blind, for the stool should be set and the gunners settled in the blind before one can really see to shoot, for this is the hour at which the blacks leave the potholes and swamps at the heads of the coves and fly either out to sea or to the center of some large body of water safely distant from any hostile shore.

The decoys are set. The gunners are in the blind. The nether cusp of the moon rests upon the horizon to the west. A saffron, pinkish light suffuses the eastern sky and dims the moon. It is a moment of sheer breathless beauty.

The hush-hush of wings high and invisible overhead tells us that the blacks are already on the move, and we become tense as our thumbs creep toward the safeties. This is really only a reflex action, for we know from experience that these high ducks are "bound," that they will not lose a wingbeat, as they sail, five hundred feet up, straight for the sea.

A flock of Canada geese far out on the pond call to each other, or perhaps to the blacks, with that wild, eerie, primeval sound, which brings to me the same neck-prickling sensation evoked by the wail of a coyote. They both speak of the lonely places unmutilated by man.

Thus, our day begins and each one of us is filled with that marvelous, tingling sensation of anticipation shared perhaps only by a ten-year-old on Christmas Eve.

As those of us who have done any gunning know only too well, an otherwise pleasant day of duck hunting can be spoiled by taking along the wrong companion to share the sport.

There has to be a first day for every duck hunter, of course, but beware of the man—or woman either, for that matter

—who talks vaguely about not having shot for years and then assumes a blank but purportedly intelligent expression in an attempt to convince you that what you are talking about is being understood. Often you will subsequently find that the sole shooting experience of this hunting aspirant has consisted of a half hour spent in a shooting gallery at Coney Island, back in 1936.

Beware also of the man who has never handled a shotgun.

Somebody has to teach the tyro, sometime, of course. I don't mind instructing him if he is frank and truthful and admits freely that he is a member in good standing of that caste. But I am truly afraid of the man who professes to have knowledge which he does not really possess.

The self-confessed tyro is not a serious problem. You have had due and constructive notice of the situation and can deal with it accordingly.

Don't take him straight to a duck blind. Get out your hand trap and throw a few clay birds for him. This will give you an opportunity to inculcate in him the rudiments of gun manners and some of the basic rules of safety.

If you have reason to doubt the accuracy of the statements of the prospective gunning companion as to his previous gunning experience, invite him for a little trap-shooting, too. Five minutes on the range will tell you volumes about what sort of gunner he will prove to be.

The true nature of a man manifests itself on a gunning expedition. If you know someone who, you consider, is in the normal course of life selfish and lazy, you will find to your regret that, while duck hunting, these two undesirable attributes become vastly more pronounced and apparent; and you alone will be setting and unsetting the decoys, rowing the boat exclusively and carrying all the heavy and unwieldy loads.

In other words, pick your gunning companion with the same care and forethought you would employ in selecting a business partner, except that in the testing, I suggest the employment of a finer mesh screen and a stronger acid.

chapter two

THE BLIND

In most types of hunting the hunter must conceal himself from the huntee. The most notable exception to this is, perhaps, upland bird shooting, where the game attempts to hide from the hunter until driven into the panic of flight either by the always-essential dog or by the hunter himself.

In duck hunting, however, except for what I term pot-hole shooting, in which a different kind of concealment is used, some sort of blind or concealment for the hunter is an essential. Ducks possess excellent vision, and it would appear that the higher the degree of edibility of a species of duck the better its vision and the greater its capacities for alarm and apprehension. The ubiquitous black duck, which I consider inferior only to the canvasback and the teal as a table delicacy—unless he has recently been gorging himself on duck clams—can be spooked into flight by a movement on the shore a quarter of a mile away.

On the other hand, the true coot—the little fellow with a bill like a crow and small paddles instead of webbing on each tarsal of his toes—can often be approached to within gunshot merely by walking out upon the shore. He is generally regarded in the same class as the crow as far as his edibility is concerned, although I think that this maligns him to a considerable extent, for he lives almost entirely on vegetable matter and, I suppose, on insects in season.

So we must have a blind.

The blind, apparently most beloved by the cartoonists, is simply a boat hidden among the reeds or cattails. In real life, however, an ideal situation in which to conceal a boat in this manner is infrequently found. Unless the reeds are very close to the boat and are well above the heads of the seated gunners, the concealment afforded is generally not adequate and unless a lot of work is done there cannot be any shielding overhead. Another drawback to using the concealed boat as a blind is the element of danger. Two gunners in a boat are either facing each other or, which is even worse, the man in the center seat of the boat has his back toward the man in the stern.

If you must use the boat as a blind—and there are circumstances, of course, in which the method cannot be avoided—be sure, in unfamiliar terrain, on tidewater, that you have reliable information on the tides. Many gunners, having found a perfect spot among the reeds with perhaps a foot of water, have had the tide run out and have spent a cold and miserable six hours or more waiting for it to come in again because they were unable to drag the heavy boat through the mud and ooze to open water.

For inland hunting on lakes, and particularly for river hunting the boat is acceptable as a blind and, in fact, can be very useful. Concealed under overhanging trees or alders at a lake or riverbank, the only drawback of the boat used as a blind is the danger of the gunners' positions with relation to each other. This can be eliminated by taking along a wide board of suitable length and placing it from bow to stern seat at one side of the boat. The boat, of course, is run aground close to and parallel to the shore. If there are no reeds or marsh grass, the offshore side of the boat can be effectively concealed by leafy branches or pine trees or cedars. The gunners thus can sit side by side facing the water.

THE FIXED BLIND

The first question to be decided about the fixed blind is, of course, its site.

Ducks, so far as I have been able to determine, do not employ regular flyways as do crows in passing back and forth from feeding grounds to rookeries; but ducks, in flying up and down coves or inlets, do seem to keep in the center and away from the shores. This appears to be the invariable rule when one is ensconced in a good blind on the shore with a tastefully arranged and generously proportioned stool set out before it.

I think that it is generally conceded that a point makes the best location for a blind—either permanent or movable. The ducks seem to come closer to the land at points and they thus can obtain a better aerial view of the decoys. Furthermore, you can see more from a point—the floor show is better—because you can enjoy that quivering, anticipatory excitement engendered by watching even those ducks who are bound, tail end to, a half mile or more away and who have not the slightest intention of coming anywhere near you.

There is one major exception to the point rule which should receive mention. If you know of a cove or a straight bit of beach near the shore of which you have observed birds feeding on eel grass or widgeon grass or wild celery or rice or similar delectable duck groceries, that might be a good place to install a sort of second line blind. A movable one would do because you will probably not get too many shots there. After the regular clients of this cafeteria have been shot at a few times they may take their patronage elsewhere; and in a location of this kind you are not apt to get much pass or flight shooting.

So probably the best location for your principal blind is the tip of a point.

The next question—if you do not own the point selected—is that of obtaining the permission of the owner thereof to

FIGURE 3 *The fixed blind. Part of dressing removed to show construction.*

FIGURE 4 *The same blind–dressing incomplete.*

use it for gunning purposes, even if it is not posted—a not-too-likely event in these days, when the making of "No Trespassing" signs is a lucrative profession.

It is desirable to obtain such permission and it should be exclusive permission, preferably in writing, lest some cold winter morning you find another group of gunners settled down on the shore close to your blind or—worse yet—actually in your blind.

I have found through the process of being both disappointed and uncomfortable—a disagreeable combination—that it is well worth while to take a little extra trouble and care in building your permanent blind. It pays off in more ducks and in more pleasure even if you plan to use the blind only five or six times during the season.

The ideal blind is built somewhat like an old-fashioned backhouse, with a shed roof and a front like a Dutch door with the top half missing. The door which you use, however, should be on the side. If possible, orient the blind so that the morning sun will not hit you square in the eyes and remember, as you build the blind—probably in October—that by December the sun is going to rise a lot farther to the south than it did on Columbus Day.

If you are on tidewater with a considerable rise and fall, your problem will be complicated and, of course, where the difference in height between flood and ebb tide is too great, a movable blind will have to be employed.

Locate the blind as near to the water's edge as possible. The range, even of the express loads, is limited, and at much over forty yards gaps begin to appear in the pattern large enough to permit your feathered objective to escape unscathed. Not being on tidewater, I usually place the front of the blind practically at the water's edge. A few feet leeway will serve to protect the blind from wind-driven ice in the event of a freeze-up and may preserve its essential structure for use next year.

How big should the blind be?

I believe that more than three gunners in a blind is dangerous and that two are better and safer than three. However,

I usually build a permanent blind to accommodate three. If you have more than one blind and each accommodates only two people, then, if the group hunting is odd in number, one man has to gun alone—a procedure which I think is inadvisable, particularly in rugged weather.

The blind should be long enough so that the butt of your gun does not prod the gunner to your right in the navel, but not so long that guns can be swung sideways dangerously. When two men are shooting in a three-man blind, the two should sit together in the center, at a comfortable distance from each other, but not so far that the right hand man, for example, may be tempted to try a ninety-degree shot to the left.

I think the best dimensions for a blind are about seven feet six inches by four feet six inches.

Ideal for the four corner posts, if you have them available, are the six-foot-length steel fence posts of T or angle-iron cross section. They are easily driven into the ground, without digging, and establish an almost permanent skeleton for your blind. Through the holes which are punched in these posts every six inches or so you can drive nails into whatever material you are going to use to sheathe the blind—old doors or batten shutters or old trash lumber will do. Of course, if you have no old steel fence posts, weathered two-by-fours or even sharpened hardwood saplings are entirely adequate, but it is well to dig a hole before you apply the sledge to their splintery tops.

The front posts should stick up about three feet above the ground—you don't want a high post to interrupt the swing of your gun if you should have to shoot sitting down—and the back posts may be left about four or more feet high. The vertical dimensions of this blind are applicable to sites where the surrounding vegetation is at least as high as the blind will be. In sites where this is not the case, the floor of the blind will have to be sunk into the ground—but not below water level, for ice makes poor footing for the gunner—and the vertical dimensions reduced accordingly.

Use only weathered lumber in the sheathing of a blind. The yellow of unweathered lumber will stand out like a stop light, even through the dressing which will be applied later. The tighter you can make the blind the more comfortable you will be come the northwest storms of late November and December. Old canvas, roofing paper, or even discarded carpeting will help a lot—particularly if you are short on suitable lumber.

Make the seat high enough!

Nothing will make your feet colder and make your knees stiffer and put a kink in your back more effectively than squatting, on a cold day, on a seat that is way too low for you. Furthermore, you'll nearly pop a blood vessel as you finally stagger and struggle to your feet when the ducks do come in.

Seventeen inches from the ground is about right for the average-sized man, and I've had no complaints on this height even from the six-foot-plussers. A seat twelve inches wide set six inches away from the back wall will be comfortable, and you won't get cramped sitting on it.

Speaking of the back wall, this should be run up so that it is about six inches higher than the tallest gunner's head when he is sitting down, and the sides should be boxed in as far as the front of the seat—thus, about eighteen inches from the back.

By all means have a roof, a short steeply pitched shed roof, slanting up toward the front of the blind. Sit in the seat when it is finished and have someone behind the blind hold a board over your head at an upward slant ending above the front of the seat. When you can get to your feet without hitting your head on the board—and you'd better clear it by four or five inches—the pitch and height are right. That is the line of your roof.

Tar paper or old canvas on the roof and down the back of the blind will keep you dry in a driving rain—except when it is straight in your face and, even then, you won't have that disagreeable sensation that the Gremlins are pouring little kettles of water down the back of your neck.

At this point, I can hear a lot of gunners getting to their feet and saying, "Hell, you can't see up in a blind like that, and you can't see behind you. It's no good."

My answer is, "It may be a lot of fun to look up and to look behind you; but if you do, and there happen to be any ducks in the air at the same time, the movement and the white flash of your face will scare them into the next county. You may get the pleasure of looking at them, but you probably won't get a shot."

Another advantage of the high back and the roof is that they put you in a shadow and eliminate silhouette—both important features when the ducks are coming in to stool. As to the ducks coming from behind, I have seen them—since they could not see me—pitch right in overhead into the stool.

Two more structural details, and then we'll get to the dressing of the blind.

ONE: make the door, which can be at one end or the other, wide enough. When you've knocked down and crippled a duck, and he lands out in the water forty or fifty yards away, you'll want to be able to get out of the blind quickly.

TWO: put a board across the front of the blind for a shelf—for shells, binoculars, the milk chocolate and the thermos. It is far better than keeping them in the mud on the floor.

DRESSING

The vegetation growing around your blind makes, of course, the best dressing.

If it's marsh grass, cut it with long hedge shears or a machete and apply it to the blind with battens of weathered wood or weave it into two-inch chicken wire and tack the wire around the blind. Don't forget the roof and the back. These must be made to look as much like the surrounding terrain as possible. If you use marsh grass, let it stick up above the front of the blind to the level of the top of your head, when seated, or even a little higher. One great advantage to this type of dressing is that you can swing your gun through it if you should have to shoot sitting, as you often do if you do not see the incoming ducks soon enough to permit you to get to your feet.

If the blind is set among alders or other deciduous bushes you cannot, of course, do a proper dressing job with dry branches. For such location I cut small pitch pines, as early in the season as possible, and tack them to the blind for dressing. They turn a neutral and acceptable brown after a few frosts.

If the site is among scrub oak or other deciduous trees, some of which retain their dried leaves for most of the fall and winter, you can use their branches although they are unco-operative stuff to handle. Cut the branches while the leaves are still green and the chances are that, after they become sere and brown, they will hang on to the branches at least for the duration of the season.

Should you be forced to put your blind out on a beach, at a distance from the flora growing on the shore, "tie" it to such vegetation by running a thin fence of similar vegetation from the blind to the nearest clump of bushes or trees so that it will appear that the blind is a part of the natural flora growing down to the shore. This can be accomplished by lashing trees and branches to a wire fence run from the blind to the natural growth. If your blind is at such a site, get out in your boat, at a distance of a hundred yards or so, before and after you "tie" the blind. You will see what I mean. The blind will no longer look like the Empire State Building; it will look like a clump of bushes at the end of a strip of them running down to the water.

Leave some extra dressing to cover your boat. If you do this you can keep the boat beside or behind the blind, and its unfriendly outline will not frighten the ducks who may plan to make a social call on your decoys.

Now that your fixed blind is completed, seat one of your fellow gunners in the blind and go out in your boat, or wade out, if you can, and look the scene over with the critical eye of a black duck. Repair gaps and round out any revealing straight lines with extra dressing to remove any suspicious or unnatural outlines.

FIGURE 5 *Another fixed blind. Note roof of tar paper and dressing on top of roof. A peep hole in side wall may be seen at left center.*

FIGURE 6 *The blind "tied" to the shore vegetation. Dressing on fence is incomplete.*

Next to the actual hunting of ducks, building a blind is one of the best parts of gunning. When a good job has been done, you will derive a pleasant feeling of satisfaction and you will look forward the more keenly to the opening of the season.

There are, of course, many other types of fixed blinds, some of which fall into the improvised class.

Some people sink a barrel—a large one—into the sand or mud and pile up a little brush or dressing around it. It's a good deal like sitting in a grave with your head sticking out; and, even if you cover the top of the barrel carefully, you may find it half full of rain water or ice on some frosty December morning. I have never used one of these, but it seems to me like unnecessary and self-inflicted punishment.

If your site comprises a bluff sloping sharply down to the water, you can make yourself a good blind by digging a deep trench below the crest to avoid a silhouette against the sky. In a well-drained sandy soil, you won't have much trouble

FIGURE 7 *Fixed blind—details of roof and side construction.*

FIGURE 8 *A closer view of the "tie" fence in process of construction.*

FIGURE 9 *Other side of "tie" fence showing open door of blind.*

with rain water; but it will not be too comfortable. A few armfuls of hay or marsh grass in the bottom will make it warmer for your feet.

I have shot from such a blind and must admit that it does fool the ducks, particularly if some care is exercised in placing dressing at the front of it. If you are on salt water, remember that seaweed piled up makes good dressing.

Even on a flat open beach a trench may be dug to conceal the gunners. Don't forget that it is about as important to build up the sand or beach grass behind you as it is to erect a concealing barrier in front of you. Silhouettes alarm ducks too.

There is another type of fixed blind which should receive some mention. This is a boxlike affair mounted on spiles out in the water some distance from the shore. Building one is hard work and, inasmuch as the ice almost invariably carries it away each winter, it has to be remade every year. In certain cases and in certain locations, the building of such a blind cannot be avoided—for example, in places where the water is very shallow for a long distance from the shore and the bottom is very light in color so that the ducks are disinclined to land or even to come close in.

If you have to build such a blind, build it, of course; but keep a few things in mind. If you are on tidewater, make the blind high enough so that it will not be flooded out on extra high tides. It is a good idea to make it high enough so that you can conceal your boat by sliding it underneath—but, again, if you are on tidewater make your calculations carefully and accurately, lest someday your boat should come up through the floor on the high tide or pull the spiles out of the bottom or just plain sink.

It is also a good idea, if practicable, to locate the blind within wading distance of the shore. In the first place it is much easier to build it when you are standing on the solid bottom than when you are teetering in an unco-operative boat. Furthermore, the use of such a blind is limited by ice conditions. For instance, three quarters of an inch of ice will not support you, and it is a terrific job to put on the "Washington Crossing the Delaware" act with the boat while trying to cut a channel from the shore to the blind. If, however, the blind is within wading distance and the ice is not too thick, you can cut a narrow channel to walk through by the judicious and not too onerous use of a square-ended garden spade—the heavier the better.

I have seen and used blinds of this type with no dressing on them at all—just the bare weathered boards exposed to the critical gaze of the ducks. They worked quite well—I did not get skunked in them—but I believe that some breaking up of the straight unnatural lines would have improved their usefulness.

Another type of blind is the concrete box set out in the water. This is, naturally, an expensive blind. Furthermore, if there has been much rain or if it has been very rough, someone has to get up at a mighty early hour in the morning and pump it out. If the temperature should drop below thirty-two degrees, the process is even more complicated and laborious. I have seen such blinds turned upside down by the ice and, in these cases, there is nothing to do but build a new one and dynamite the old one.

I don't recommend concrete blinds out in the water. They might be all right on shore, but none of us is going to live forever.

MOVABLE BLINDS

I think the best and most easily handled movable blind is made of that light three-foot wire garden fencing in which the vertical wires run like inverted U's and are bound together with twisted horizontal wires.

Twelve to fifteen feet of this is sufficient. Weave marsh grass or hay into it, letting the dressing protrude about a foot at the top. Roll the whole thing up, tie it with a bit of string, and you have a somewhat cumbersome but light and easily transportable blind. It can be quickly set out on the beach or marsh in a roughly eliptical shape and the downward pointing legs of the U's can be pushed into the sand or mud to brace it. A few oak boughs with spreading branches placed at the back will serve as a roof for purposes of concealment.

You will need seats. Old-fashioned, wooden beer cases with the partitions knocked out are ideal when set on end to obtain sufficient height. Further, they can be employed to carry shells and other impedimenta to and from the hunting site. A diagonal brace across the open side will make them more rigid and also act as a handle for carrying.

It is well to take a spade or a long-handled shovel with you on an expedition of this kind because, if your blind is too conspicuous and stands up too high, you may want to dig a trench to lower it a bit. Then dig a trench for your feet and turn your beer cases on their sides to lower them, too.

Another type of movable blind can readily be constructed out of four one-by-two-inch wood frames with one diagonal brace, two of the frames three feet by six feet and two of them about four by three feet. These can be fastened together at the corners by ordinary hooks and eyes to form a rectangular pen. The frames can be covered with cut up burlap bags or old discarded canvas of a neutral shade. This type is more cumbersome and heavier than the wire blind and may not blend in with the background as well.

IMPROVISED BLINDS

Each one of these depends upon the local situation as you find it and therefore only a few general statements can be made about them.

In many instances where the improvised blind is used, you will have no boat. Thus, unless the wind is in a direction which will blow dead birds in to you or to some shore where you can retrieve them, go somewhere else. It is a form of murder to kill birds which are not picked up for eating.

Beach shooting or shooting on sand spits usually involves setting up some kind of improvised concealment for the gunner.

FIGURE 10 *The movable blind partially unrolled. This grass and wire blind is the lightest and handiest type.*

FIGURE 11 *Detail of wire and woven grass movable blind.*

Where there is beach grass he can dig a small foxhole which will conceal him fairly effectively. Frequently no decoys are employed and–if there are several gunners–a location or series of locations are chosen, where it is known that the birds fly back and forth. Again, don't shoot on an offshore wind when the birds cannot be retrieved.

POTHOLE HUNTING

This is one of the most interesting and delightful forms of duck hunting.

A pothole, according to my definition, is a very small pond, measured in feet or yards, or a swamp with some open pools or the narrow head of some cove. Some rivers lend themselves to this type of hunting.

Fundamentally there must be cover for your stalking, for if the surrounding countryside is bare and open, you might just as well go home and keep warm by the fire.

The native black duck, particularly, is fond of potholes. As far as I can observe, he usually enters them about dusk and if there is feed, will stay there until late the next morning. In fact I've found blacks, mallards, and teal in potholes at all times of day. All the so-called pond and river, or dabbling ducks, like them.

It is difficult to pothole hunt alone. Depending upon the lay of the land and the size and shape of the pothole in question, it is advisable to have anywhere from three to five gunners along. Experience with each place will teach you which way the flushed ducks will fly out on which wind. These routes may often lie up a draw, between two hills or ridges; but most often if there is a brook or water lead running into or out of the pothole, they will follow that.

Minutes in advance of the time anyone goes down near the pothole, the gunners–except for the "scarer-outer"–should make their respective ways quietly to these probable flyways and so place themselves that they are concealed as well as possible from any bird flying away from the pothole. After you have shot a hole a few times, you will know how long it takes the fellow who has the farthest to travel to get into position. Time it with your watch, not by guesswork.

When each man is in position, the "scarer-outer" proceeds cautiously and as quietly as possible to the pothole. If it is practicable, he will move upwind. Many claim that ducks have a well-developed sense of smell. I don't know whether they have or not, but anyone knows that sound travels better downwind. If you are fortunate, it has been raining and the leaves are soft, pliable and noiseless beneath your feet. Snow is a silencer too, but the ducks will probably see you sooner because of the contrast of your dark bulk moving upon it.

If the cover is very thick, it is a wise precaution to cut a rudimentary trail to the water before the season opens. This increases the chances of the "scarer-outer" to get a shot. That's not being a hog either, for I have seen more than a dozen ducks fly out of a pothole not much bigger than a two-car garage.

FIGURE 12 *Is anyone here?*

When, from time to time, you stop to peer through the brush, always have yourself in a position from which you can shoot quickly. In other words, stop with your left foot ahead of your right, gun in both hands, thumb behind, but *not* on the safety (you might trip), index finger of right hand at the right hand forward edge of trigger guard, but *not* on the trigger.

The actual shooting will be left for another chapter, but we can mention here that this type of hunting successfully combines the charms of water fowling and upland shooting. For the men up on the hill ahead of you it is a wonderful thrill to see a pair of blacks or mallards as big as two B-29's beating over the top of a pine tree.

Two further suggestions for this type of hunting. First, if you knock a duck down in the brush, go to him immediately. Both the black and the mallard—unlike sea ducks—are at home on land and they can both run and hide well and their coloration is highly protective, particularly in the case of the black. A dog is useful here, and even with hound dogs I have found blacks in heavy cover.

Second, if the pothole is bare of ducks—or appears to be —make a loud sharp noise. Ducks sometimes hide, or try to hide, until you get quite close to them, and often they have to be shocked into flight. I once fired several times at a pothole from a vantage point near an anticipated flyway and then, on my way back to the car, kicked up a black who had not taken to wing even at the shots, less than a hundred yards away.

A final word on comfort in the blind in cold climates.

This may sound effete, but I believe that the more comfortable you are in a blind, the better and more accurate your shooting will be. A small portable charcoal stove or brazier will help a great deal to keep you comparatively comfortable and flexible when the wind is northwest and the temperature is sulking down around ten or twenty degrees.

An old-fashioned carriage warmer will do—if you have one in the attic—although it is a little too small to perform a really good job; or you can make a good and efficient stove in half an hour or so.

Take an old ten-quart bucket and punch a liberal number of holes in the bottom and in the sides within two or three inches of the bottom. Unless you have a grate, it won't last too long, for the bottom will burn out. If you don't have an old broken piece of cast-iron stove grate, you can make a passable one by weaving and bending telephone or fence wire into a mat two or three inches thick and a little smaller than the bottom of the bucket. The grate holes do not have to be very small because you'll probably use charcoal briquettes anyway.

Start the fire with kerosene or paper, keeping the bucket outside the blind. When the charcoal is glowing well, bring the bucket inside and either set it up on flat stones to provide bottom draft, or scoop out a trench a few inches deep and set the bucket over it.

A few words of warning and advice:

Have on hand a piece of stiff wire a foot or so long with a hook at each end to use in lifting the bucket by its bail. It will be too hot to handle even with gloves. Make a snug cover for the bucket out of mosquito netting; hardware cloth may lose its solder from the heat. The cover is to keep things—particularly live shells—from falling into your miniature inferno. A shell dropped into glowing charcoal will not delay long before it explodes.

This simple contraption will go a long way toward keeping you comfortable and in an uncongealed condition.

chapter three

DUCK DECEPTION

Why do ducks come in to decoys?

It may be hunger, it may be sex, or it may be sheer gregariousness.

Hunger may play a considerable part in it. If you set your decoys over light-colored bottom in shallow water where obviously there is no feed, the ducks will not come in as readily as they will over a dark bottom which holds the promise of some nourishment.

Sex is probably a very small part. In the first place ducks do not breed in the fall—although I have seen recently hatched baby ducks as late as September. I have also, many times, seen a hen mallard—I breed both mallards and blacks—doing the love dance, or rather love swim, around a drake on a cold blustery December day after she had had her daily ration of whole corn. The drake, however, was utterly apathetic; as far as he was concerned, she might as well have been another drake. So it probably isn't sex.

Gregariousness, I think, is the dominating impulse. You have probably noticed that, broadly speaking, most of the ducks which drop down right in the middle of your decoys—as contrasted with looking them over from a height of fifty feet—come in singly or in pairs. They are probably lonely and welcome the opportunity to join this "Marching and Munching Society" which is bobbing so peacefully upon the waves. I am not sure that this conclusion leads to anything, however, because I really do not know how to set a stool so as to appeal to a duck's gregarious instincts—and I don't believe that anyone else does either, although there have been reams written about the setting of decoys. There are a few do's and don'ts to be observed, which I shall deal with later, but I do not think that the art of setting decoys is nearly as complex as some of the writers for the sport magazines claim.

There are five principal types of decoys:

1. The old-fashioned wooden block
2. The cork decoy
3. The molded-paper or plastic decoy
4. The rubber decoy
5. The shadow

I once saw another type—a stuffed decoy made of real duck feathers with a quacker inside, operated from the blind by a bulb and a long tube running from the bulb to the quacking mechanism. They sold—if they did—for about thirty-five dollars apiece. I haven't seen one in some time and don't know how successful they were—but my doubts are more than serious. They always seemed to me to be the kind of Christmas present that a non-duck hunter would send to that best customer who is an avid duck hunter, but who never touches a drop. But to return to the more standard and within-everyone's-reach decoys.

The wooden block decoy is heavy, very heavy.

If you engage in peripatetic duck hunting and wander from one gunning site to another, the wooden blocks are not your answer. Burdened with gun and gunning bag, you cannot carry more than about six of these decoys unless you are an iron man. The pressed paper ones, and more particularly the rubber ones, will answer your needs much better. You can stuff half a dozen rubber decoys into a capacious pocket and hardly know that you are carrying them.

The wooden decoy, however, is unexcelled for use at a fixed blind. It can take more punishment than any of the others and, inasmuch as you have to cart them only twice—at the beginning and at the end of the season, provided you live in an honest community—their weight does not present a serious problem. Shotgun pellets may chip them, but they won't sink them. They can be dragged over stony shores if reasonable care is used not to break the heads off. The neck is really the only vulnerable part. The wooden decoy is usually smooth and, if you undertake to repaint him yourself, be sure that you use the dullest, flattest paint you can buy. The sun does not glint and reflect from real ducks, and it should not do so from your decoys.

The cork decoys are, in some ways, an improvement over the wooden blocks. They are usually made in a mold of ground-up cork held together with a binder of some kind. They have three principal advantages. First, of course, their lightness, for they weigh only a fraction of what the wooden decoy weighs. In the second place, they have a rough stippled surface, which prevents sun glints even when they are wet. However, a flat paint should be used on them, too. Thirdly, they share the advantage of the wooden block, in that they are relatively undamaged by gun pellets. When it comes to dragging them on a rough shore, they are considerably more fragile than their wooden brethren. However, if I were buying new decoys for use at a fixed blind, I think I would get the cork type. Some of my tendons stay partially pulled all winter from moving one hundred and fifty-odd wooden blocks twice each fall.

The pressed-paper or plastic decoy is lighter even than the cork. They are so light, in fact, that, it seems to me they bob about unnaturally if the water is at all rough. They have the advantage of the stippled finish and inasmuch as most of them have the dye right in them they do not have to be repainted. Their weakness is that they are very vulnerable to shot wounds. After a few number fours or number sixes have passed through him, pal paper decoy develops an alcoholic list to starboard. If there are not too many holes in him, and you can learn to finger these, as one would a flute, you can blow the water out of him

FIGURE 13 *The stool set and blind removed. It had been behind the goose decoys on shore. Note gap of open water in stool in front of blind site.*

FIGURE 14 *The same set photographed from one side in the water. Note gap in front of shadow decoy.*

FIGURE 15 *A conference of veteran wooden blocks. Goldeneye and scaup.*

FIGURE 16 *Another huddle of the same species with a redhead at left.*

FIGURE 17 *Drake goldeneye wooden block registering surprise.*

FIGURE 18 *Now past the half-century mark, this old Canada goose block lends an air of respectability to the set stool.*

and patch up the holes with Ambroid or Duco cement. However, one does not get much time to run a decoy hospital during the gunning season, and the fewer such tasks you set for yourself the more time you will have for gunning.

Decoys of all three types I place, five to a string, on a stout line about twenty-seven feet long, or a little longer if the water is deep. Light sash cord is good.

There is no benefit in signalling to the incoming ducks that each decoy is shackled by a bright, white cord, so, before I use a cord, I coil it in an old bucket and pour in a mixture of about a quarter of a pint of green stain or paint thinned with kerosene or turpentine, which will dry more quickly. I swizzle this around a bit with a stick, leaving the top end of the cord tied to the bail so it can be located again, then I pull the whole line out on the ground and let it dry.

Anchors should be placed at each end of the line. I prefer the mushroom type made of lead with a piece of heavy wire in the form of a loop cast into it. These are not difficult to make yourself if you have a lead kettle, a ladle and a box with sand in it to make the molds. Bend the wire in the form of a U, then bend each leg of the U inward or outward for about three quarters of an inch to secure good anchorage in the lead. An anchor three inches in diameter and an inch deep is sufficient, and you can use a good-sized orange to make your original impression in the sand. After that you can use the anchor which you have just made and can eat the orange.

Six feet of cord from the anchor to the first decoy is usually sufficient for most locations, but if you are going into deeper water make the line longer.

I used to put three-foot trolls out from the main cord to each decoy. However, I don't do this any more because of the tendency of such a rig to get tangled and fouled with other strings of decoys if the anchors drag a little on a stormy day. Now, I merely cast five loops in the line at three-foot intervals (which leaves about six feet of line between the last decoy

FIGURE 19 *The mushroom type anchor. This clings well to the bottom and will drag very little even in rough weather.*

FIGURE 20 *The only virtue of this type of anchor is that it can be slipped over the head of a decoy when not in use. On any kind of bottom it drags too readily.*

and the second anchor) and fasten the screw eye of a decoy to each loop.

By trial and a great deal of error, I think I have found a good way in which to attach the decoy to the loop in the cord. I go into this at some length because there is nothing more irritating than having to chase a decoy which has come adrift, while all the bluebills within three miles are trying to pay a visit to your stool.

The old-fashioned decoys used to be made with a leather loop on the bow end of the bottom. This was good because the leather would not cut the lashing between it and the line loop on the main cord. However, leather rots out after a few years, and it is difficult to get pieces of leather to replace it. So I used a heavy brass screw eye. Then I tried cod line to fasten the loop to the screw eye; but the screw eye chafed the line apart before

FIGURE 21 *A sound method of attaching the decoy to the line. Note leather strad.*

the season was over. Now I get from a fishing-tackle store little strips of leather about three eighths of an inch wide and two and a half inches long, with a hole bored in each end, which fishermen use to connect their surf rigs to their lines. Pass one end through the loop and the screw eye and tie the ends together with cod line threaded through the two holes in the ends of the leather. This method reduces the trouble with errant decoys by more than half. Of course, these leathers will rot out too, after two or three seasons' use, but they are much easier to replace than the strip of leather fastened to the bottom of the decoy inself.

The only type of rubber decoy with which I am familiar is the self-inflating kind. This decoy has an inverted rubber chimney extending downward from its belly for about six inches, around the lower end of which is inserted an iron ring. To set the decoy, hold it by bill and tail with two hands, so that there will be as much air in its collapsed, balloonlike carcass as possible, and level it so that the iron ring at the bottom of the chimney is parallel to the surface of the water and an inch or two above it. Then drop the decoy. As the iron ring tends to sink the decoy, the air in the chimney is forced up into the body of the decoy itself, which inflates and assumes the shape of a duck. Due to the keel action of the chimney and the ballast of the iron ring, these decoys are fairly stable and steady. They have a wrinkled surface simulating feathers, and thus do not glint in the sunlight. Their principal drawback is that a moderate wind will distort their shapes and make unnatural dents in them. They are really best in calm or moderately calm waters.

A gun pellet will, naturally, sink one immediately; but I suppose that they could be hot or cold patched on the inside. I haven't had to try to fix one.

Two suggestions as to this kind of decoy:

String them singly with one anchor for each—or, at the most, put two on an anchor. If you have any more than that, inasmuch as you will have to use both hands to set each one, the others will fill with water and perhaps sink while you are setting one. Then you have to haul them up one by one, and empty the water out of them. While you are doing that, you may, if the line between the decoys is not long enough, lift one which you have already set and let some of his air escape. He will immediately assume the aspect of a duck in the last stages of botulism and you will have to lift him up, drain him and reset him.

The rubber decoys which I have used are equipped with a rubber knob cast onto the breast, which the manufacturer placed there as a sort of cleat to which the anchor line may be attached. I find that these knobs wear out in a season or two—and, of course, if they break off or develop a crack, the decoy will sink. So I tie the anchor line to the iron ring at the bottom of the chimney. The decoys don't head into the wind so well with this rig, but why should they? You'll have more variety in your stool if they don't.

This type of decoy is ideal for situations in which you have to walk a long way to your blind and cannot or do not want to leave the decoys at the blind overnight. It is also perfect for what I call a "duck crawl" in which you go from one site to another, and stand or sit in the bushes, after throwing out a few decoys. Unless the ducks come in, you plan to stay only half an hour or so before moving on to another spot. As I have said before, you can stuff half a dozen of these decoys in your pocket and barely be aware that you are carrying them.

The shadow is a very useful decoy, particularly for black ducks and particularly in the dim uncertain light of dawn. He also used to be valuable at dusk before the government changed the rules on us.

This decoy consists of an oversized representation of a duck—usually a black—cut out of a three-quarter-inch board. The figure has a flat bottom representing the water line. In order to give him apparent bulk, when viewed from either the front or the rear, two quarter circles of the same sort of board are fastened—one on each side—at right angles to the body and at about the center, measured fore and aft. The radius of the

FIGURE 22 *The rubber decoy in a relaxed mood.*

FIGURE 23 *Setting the rubber decoy. Drop him into the water from this position.*

quarter circles is equal to the height of the body at the point at which they are attached. This rig is painted, two or three coats, with dull, flat, black paint. It is then mounted on a circular or square platform which has been painted a dull water green. The dimensions of these platforms are usually about eighteen inches in diameter or sixteen to eighteen inches square. Rectangular platforms are not so good. They are more apt to tip over.

You can make these shadows yourself, but one word of warning. The specific gravity of wood varies a great deal, depending on the species of tree and upon the extent of the kiln drying. Therefore, before you permanently attach the decoy to the platform, test him out on a sample platform to be sure he is stable and will not change into an underwater cormorant at the first puff of wind. I have found that the circular platform, although more trouble to make, seems to be more seaworthy. The anchor line should be fastened to the platform; if attached at different points on different decoys, you will have a greater variety in the positions of your shadows as regards their angles to the wind.

These shadows sometimes perform miracles with black ducks, and I always have four or five of them at each blind.

I was on a marsh once at high noon in a snowstorm. One gunner had three shadows set out in a small puddle, some ten feet in diameter and not a foot deep. He was sitting about ten yards from the puddle on a little tussock and was only partially concealed by the surrounding marsh grass.

A single black duck came in and hovered, like an osprey, over the three decoys. Mr. Gunner fired and missed and the black circled for about two hundred yards and tried to come in again. On the second time around, Mr. Gunner was too eager and fired when the range was about fifty yards or more. He missed again. The black wheeled wide and then came in for the third time, and Mr. Gunner got him.

I once had two blacks hover over my shadows. I knocked down one with the right barrel, and the second duck continued to hover until I killed him, too. Again it was snowing.

FIGURE 24 *An old shadow decoy—the nemesis of the black duck—particularly the red-leg.*

FIGURE 25 *The same. The cleats on the neck are a repair job.*

There definitely is a magic about the shadows in certain lights and under certain conditions.

If you are going after black ducks—and who isn't in the East?—take a few shadows along. They are cumbersome and unwieldy but for some reason which I have never been able to fathom, they often give wonderful results.

SETTING THE STOOL

As I have indicated before, a great deal has been written about various methods of setting decoys. I do not decry these earnest efforts to reduce to an art or a science this fundamental aspect of duck hunting; but based upon my far from extensive experience, which does not run back into the days "when the ducks blackened the skies," I am not so sure that some of the finer points proposed by the artists of decoy setting are really so important after all.

An old gunning friend of mine, who brought down his first canvasback well before the turn of the century used to claim that ducks decoyed about as well to a bunch of gallon oil tins, painted a dull black and strung on a line with an anchor at one end, as they did to the most perfectly carved decoys set in a half moon or a circle or a cross or what have you.

I guess he was right, because he was a highly truthful old man who has long since joined the thousands of ducks and geese which he shot. However, between the two extremes—the decoy technicians and my old friend—I think there is a middle ground comprised of some principles which seem to be worth while observing.

First, how many decoys should you use?

Well, back around the days of market gunning when you could hire an expert gunner for a dollar or two a day to set your decoys, take care of the live decoys, row the boat after the cripples and wipe your eye when you missed a duck, big stools were in high favor. They may have been necessitated by the fact that ducks were vastly more numerous then and

FIGURE 26 *Shadow, wooden blocks and rubber decoys. Note tipping and denting of rubber decoys, which demonstrates that they are poor even in light wind, which, on this day, was less than 10 m.p.h.*

FIGURE 27 *One end of a good decoy set. Blind is at left just out of picture. The above set is repeated in reverse at left of blind, leaving gap of open water directly in front of blind.*

traveled in much larger flocks. Thus, perhaps, it took a stool with an enormous membership to attract them.

In those days one could buy a couple of good decoys for a dollar, while today an equivalent decoy will cost you between three and four dollars. Thus, except for the extremely well to do, the big stool is out. Furthermore, most duck hunters do their own chores today. They have to, with a gunner charging from ten to fifteen dollars a day for his services and extra for the use of any of his equipment. Lastly, it takes a long time to set one or two hundred decoys, and it is a lot of work, particularly if the bottom drops off steeply and you have to set from a boat.

At my main blind, which is at the tip of a long point with a mile-wide stretch of water in front of it, I use about fifty decoys—not including four or five shadows and five or six goose blocks, just to lend an air of respectability to the aggregation. At my other blinds, which lie on subsidiary points about the sides of the main point, I use about thirty decoys and a few shadows. I often wish that I owned more decoys.

Frankly, I cannot differentiate between the results obtained with fifty decoys and the results I used to get, some years back, when I used only thirty at my main blind. Some days the urge for companionship—or whatever the urge is—seems to drive the ducks into the stool, and on the other days it would seem that there must be a "Scarlet Fever" sign in duck language hung on the front of the blind.

The direct answer to how many decoys should be used probably still is the more decoys the better. You have doubtless observed how a flock of a couple of hundred live ducks sitting on the water out in the bay will compete, entirely too successfully, with your much smaller stool. The limitations are the number of decoys you own and the time and trouble consumed in setting them.

How far off shore should the stool be set?

The question might be asked more accurately if it read, "How far from the *blind* should the stool be set?"

There are two schools of thought on this subject—the near setters and the far setters.

The far setters declare that ducks are less suspicious if the stool is pretty far out, say thirty or more yards. I maintain that a duck with suspicions tastes just as good as one without them, and that an unsuspicious duck out of gunshot has no flavor at all. Ducks seldom wheel between the decoys and the shore.

In comparing duck shooting to the standard trapshooting setup, it might be mentioned that, in the case of the latter, the platform and the trap are separated by a distance of sixteen yards. Increase this distance by only eight yards, and you can be quite sure that whatever your score was at sixteen yards, it will be reduced by probably a third. Even the experts—those who shoot in the upper nineties—might break only eighty. The main reason for this is that the greater the range the larger the gaps in the shot pattern.

Get yourself a few dozen pattern targets—a double-spread sheet of newspaper will do—and measure the gaps at thirty, forty and fifty yards. We shall treat with them in more detail in a later chapter.

There is another factor which increases the odds against the duck hunter as compared to the trapshooter, namely, the element of surprise.

The trapshooter has his gun to shoulder. He elects when the bird shall be released by calling "Pull." He knows just where the bird is coming from, and he knows that the angle of flight will lie within certain limits.

The duck hunter knows none of these things. He is probably engaged in lighting a cigarette or unwrapping the milk chocolate when his partner whispers, "Hold it!" He has to halt the motor reflexes of what he is doing at the moment, grab his gun and locate the duck or ducks, all in a split second; but all the trap shooter had to do was to say, "Pull."

Now birds who are interested in a stool will fly over it or just beyond it. Often they land beyond it and swim in to

FIGURE 28 *Don't set a string of decoys in a straight line this way.*

FIGURE 29 *Set them in a curve this way, by dropping the anchor close behind the end decoy.*

it. Thus the further away your stool is the more obstacles to success you are stacking up for yourself.

I think that the stool should be set at between fifteen and twenty yards *from the blind*. This means, as I have said before, that the blind should be as close to the water as is practical, so that the decoys will not be set too close to the shore. As a matter of fact, closeness to the shore does not seem to make so much difference in the stool's attraction for singles and pairs. It is the snarls of five or ten that seem to be more suspicious.

In what shape should the stool be set?

Here I hope that I do not offend too many stool scientists.

The principal purpose of the stool, outside of attracting ducks to it, is to slow down their flight as they pass over it.

I think that a stool should be set in whatever way it can be most easily picked up by the incoming bird. For example, you are shooting, let us say, on the end of a point which runs in the direction from which most of the birds seem to come.

FIGURE 30 *Time to go home.*

Set the stool across the point so that the incoming bird will get a view of the decoys in company front formation and not in single file.

But how about the wind?

Ducks generally do not admire rough water; but if there is feed under it, they'll take it. Many times, I have seen blacks or mallards feeding on duck clams on a lee shore in a foot of water, with the waves breaking right over them. However, if your point offers a lee, set the stool in the calmer water, if it is within reasonable gunshot.

If there is any wind to speak of, ducks will almost invariably land upwind—which means at the head or upwind end of the stool. Thus, if the wind is blowing from the right of your blind, set the stool somewhat to the left of center so that the landing strip will not be too far to the right of the blind. Right shots are difficult enough anyway without making them harder.

It seems to be definitely bad taste in duck protocol to touch or splash another duck in landing on the water. I don't think that I have ever seen an incoming duck touch a decoy when he landed. In the light of this theory, I usually split my stool in two and leave an opening of clear water some ten or twelve yards wide, directly in front of the blind. Very often the ducks will land in this blank space, particularly if it is not too windy.

Let us say that you are setting thirty decoys under the conditions of wind outlined above and that the decoys are strung in groups of five. I would put two strings at right angles to the shore on each side of the opening in front of the blind and then run the remaining two strings upwind and downwind, i.e., parallel to the shore, from each of the two groups of ten blocks so placed. A few shadows in near shore and, if you have them, a few goose blocks set at the water's edge, add immeasurably to the general decor.

In setting a string of decoys don't just walk out from shore with one end of the line in your hand and then drop it in the water when you think you have reached the proper distance. The main reason for having an anchor at each end of the string is to enable you to set and keep the string in a curve rather than in an unnatural straight line. Thus, when you get out the correct distance from the blind, turn and drop your anchor beside the first decoy in the line behind you. This will allow the string of blocks to assume a curved line, which I think looks much better and less artificial. Don't set the strings too close together. You want to create the illusion of a large number of ducks.

I might mention two additional tricks with decoys, both designed to delude the ducks. One I have tried, but the other, in order to cover myself as did Herodotus, I must admit I have been told about. Both, I think, are worth trying.

This one, I have used at a fixed blind.

To a fairly heavy anchor—two or three bricks lashed together will do—fasten a small sheave with a swivel eye at the top. A bronze sheave would be best because the galvanized ones will deteriorate quickly even in fresh water. Thread a long line—a hundred or a hundred and twenty feet through the sheave—being sure the line is large enough so that it will not slip off the pulley and jam between the wheel and the frame. Use a neutral-colored line, or dye it in the manner previously suggested for decoy lines. Knot the two ends of the line together and where the knot is located tie one or two big decoys about two or three feet apart, or a shadow. Put one end of the now doubled line in the blind, take the anchor out in the water to a point where the doubled line will be slack upon the bottom, and drop it. You may want to buoy it with a small stick or cork in case the line breaks.

Now, by pulling on one line or the other, you can make these decoys, or the shadow, swim back and forth. Out at the anchor end of their travel you can, by tugging gently at the line, make the decoy dip down and forward as if it were feeding. (One of the things which has always bothered me a little about a stool is the immobility of its members. True, with a wind, they bob up and down like gandy dancers on an old-fashioned hand-car; but unlike them, they don't go anywhere.)

I tried the above-mentioned scheme for only a part of one season in the middle of which some ten-thumbed friend of mine fouled up the lines and we did not take the time to fix them. The clinical evidence in favor of this stunt is thus not extensive. It brought in ducks a few times while we had it operating, and I think that it is worth further experiment.

As a last suggestion on this—if you want to take the trouble to obviate fouling of the lines—make a second anchor and sheave, pass the line which does not carry the decoys through that sheave and sink it off to one side, well off the straight line from the blind to anchor number one. A third sheave inside the blind also helps to avoid this difficulty.

The other idea, which I have not tried, but shall, is to attach to the breast of a decoy a small weight on the end of a string, about a foot or eighteen inches long. This, of course, is in addition to the anchor. Inasmuch as the buoyancy of each decoy varies, you will have to experiment with the size of the weight until you find the one which—according to what they tell me—will make the decoy dip its head as if it were feeding, when it bobs in the waves.

I'm going to try this myself next year.

One final word about decoys: If you are leaving them at the blind site for use on another day, by all means arrange them neatly, each string separate from the others. There is nothing more irritating than having to untangle decoys in the dark on a cold, bitter morning. They are best arranged, perhaps, in platoon front facing the water. In this position, if they are frozen to the dirt or to the sand, you will have to break out but one decoy at a time, as you pull on the line, and the momentum of each decoy moved will assist in dislodging the next. If you try to pull on a string of frozen decoys laid out in a straight line, with the cord taut between them, you may break or weaken the cord.

DUCK LANGUAGE

There are a great variety of duck calls on the market, and most of them put me in mind of an infamous Whoopee Pillow of the Gay Twenties being operated by a two-hundred-pound victim.

Some duck calls are not too bad, but the best of them must be operated with skill and taste.

In the first place, you cannot blow a call the way you would blow a New Year's Eve horn favor after the eighth drink. The call should be operated by holding it in the left hand and touching it gently to the lips. Don't try to swallow it or you will fill it all up with saliva and then it won't work. Cover the opening with the right hand and start and stop each duck word by tipping this hand away from the opening and then closing it again. Don't blow with your cheeks; push the air from your diaphragm. If you play any of the brasses or a woodwind, you will understand what I mean.

Carry the call in its box at all times lest a bit of tobacco or pocket fluff get into it and jam it at just the moment when you want it most.

Buy a duck-call record if you want to get into this art seriously; but it may be inadvisable to do that unless you have a heated garage in which to practice or unless your wife is going away to visit relatives for a week or two.

FIGURE 31 *This does not look like a duck, but if you blow it correctly it sounds like one.*

After you believe that you have made some progress, go out in the woods or fields with some gunning friend, if you have one who is close to the borders of the lunatic fringe, get about two hundred yards away from him–upwind–and play your concerti and cadenzas. If he reports that you sound like a duck, take the call with you when you go into the blind. If his comments are caustic and, perhaps vulgar, leave it home. You're not a duck caller.

Of course, any kind of duck calling, good or bad, has some entertainment value as far as your companions are concerned, even if it does not cause pleasurable palpitations among the ducks. On dull days, when the shooting is poor, it has been known to warm both the hearts and the feet of gunners.

VOICE CALLING

Some few people have the gift of calling ducks with their own voices, without having to utilize any mechanism. The art requires much practice–provided you have the ability at all –and the services of some patient friend to listen from time to time at a distance and criticize your efforts.

I can make a fair duck call by forcing air between the side of my tongue and the gum at the back of my upper jaw from which some calloused dentist removed a cherished molar thirty-odd years ago. I say that it is fair; at least my half-wild breeding ducks shout with glee as they hear it in the late afternoon when I do down to the pond to feed them. However, that may simply be what the psychologists term a conditioned reflex in which my call stimulates the duck salivary glands. Had I been ringing a bell for the past several years just before feeding time, the response to that sound might be just as enthusiastic. Wild ducks will reply to my call, but I have not had much success in inducing them to come to me.

In a later chapter, you will find some data as to which ducks talk and which do not. Suffice it to say here that only the females of certain species quack. The mallard and black drakes merely utter a low, hoarse, "greep, greep"–a difference in vocal performance for which homo sapiens is also distinguished.

chapter four

THE BOAT

Usually, when duck hunting, you employ whatever boat you already have, or can borrow from someone else. This means that your water transportation generally constitutes a compromise with the ideal.

Just for fun, however, let's treat with the ideal for a moment, or rather with the various ideals applicable to different gunning locations.

If you are going to be on bold water, where the wind gets a running start on you, or on a salt-water bay or inlet where the seas can really build up, a good stout boat with plenty of freeboard is most desirable. Furthermore, it should be a boat capable of carrying two men easily without submerging the Plimsoll line. Ten feet long is the absolute minimum for such a boat, and eleven or even twelve is better.

Don't have one man row the boat from the middle seat while the other sits in the stern. This mistake pushes the bow way up in the air where the wind will act on it as if it were a sail, while the stern sinks down to a dangerously reduced freeboard. Rowing before the wind in this position, with a following sea, can result in a swamping, and you may be offered the dubious privilege of practicing the contortion act of getting your boots and coat off while under water.

If this does happen to you, for God's sake stick to the boat. Even if the land looks close, don't attempt to swim for it in your gunning rig.

To alleviate the temptation to commit this error of putting all the load aft, I rig my boats with two sets of row-locks–one for the middle seat and one for the bow. Thus if a duck comes down dead a short distance out, on a moderately calm day when the waves don't tend to conceal him from you, one man can occupy the middle seat and can go out alone. If there are a couple of cripples far out, let two men go–one to row and one to shoot–although it is well to take two guns because it increases your fire power. Always take a gun when you go out in the boat. I have had ducks fly twenty feet over me when I didn't have one.

I usually put an extra pair of oars in a boat which is at a bold water location.

Let us suppose that it is a fairly rough day with a nice raw northwest wind. You may be alone in the boat or, if you are wise, you may have someone with you. About a hundred yards from the shore, which is to windward–if it were to leeward you would have waited in the blind for the wind to bring the duck in–you draw alongside the dead duck. Your hands are numb, your tail is wet and is slipping on the frost on the boat seat. You pull the oars inboard a way, but perhaps not enough; you make a grab for the duck; your forearm slips off the oar, which it is holding down. The oar slides into the water through the lock, or maybe a wave knocks it out of the lock.

The boat and you have a high wind resistance and the oar, lying flat in the water has, substantially, zero resistance. So you turn around on the center seat, if you are alone, or hand the remaining oar to your companion if you are not, and a clumsy paddling process with the remaining oar begins. If you are alone, don't get into the stern seat to paddle. This will raise the bow of the boat, you will head downwind immediately and you will find that the bow in this position will serve as a splendid ballooner.

By now, you will be surprised to observe that you are, without effort, traveling at almost two knots downwind and that the errant oar has, in the short space of twenty seconds, apparently moved fifty or sixty feet away.

As the nineteenth-century novelists used to say, we shall draw a curtain over this sad scene to spare the gentle reader.

If you'd only had a spare oar.

The other advantage to an extra pair of oars is that, if you have another man in the boat and get blown far downwind, both of you can row.

One of the best boats for gunning, I have found, is the fiber-glass boat. I have one in the eleven-foot size. It is light; two men can pick it up and carry it, and one man can drag it by himself without developing a hernia.

Incidentally when dragging boats, always pull them by the stern. The narrow bow acts as a skid and reduces the friction with the ground. If there is no way for a solo boat dragger to grab the stern by its center, fasten a short bridle of one-half-inch or three-quarter-inch rope to each side of the rear seat or to the stern. It should be of such length that when you stand nearly upright with the bridle in your hand the stern of the boat is off the ground.

The fiber-glass boat handles well—although I could ask for a little more keel on it, inasmuch as is spins rather readily—and it is reasonably rugged, if decent care is employed in its treatment. Of course, if it gets a hole stove in it, a major operation is involved in fixing it. I imagine that it might have to go back to the factory. I am quite careful, when the weather gets cold, to turn it over when I leave it. I don't know how well it would withstand the strain of expanding ice if a freeze came after a heavy rain.

In turning any boat over, be sure to unship the oarlocks first. Many a good boat has been strained or split by not observ-

FIGURE 32 *A good bold water boat. Note presence of oar locks at both bow and center seats.*

FIGURE 33 *The fiber-glass boat. Light and sturdy enough if handled with reasonable care.*

ing this precaution. The oarlocks should be made captive with cod line or marlin.

I find with wooden boats that the old ones do better if you have a little water in them. It keeps the planking swelled. Too much may strain them, however, when it freezes, and, in any event, it is unpleasant getting in and out of a boat when the inside of the bottom is sheathed in ice. Thus, if you have a new boat that is well caulked and tight, you can probably leave it turned over for the duration of the gunning season without developing bad leaks.

Keep a bailing can in each boat you use. An empty one pound coffee can does very nicely.

Fasten a twelve- or fifteen-foot painter to each boat. It comes in handy at odd times. If you row downwind along a

FIGURE 34 *Rope bridle at stern of boat to facilitate dragging boat. Bridle should be a little shorter than the one in picture.*

shore after a cripple or dead bird, it is far easier to walk back in six inches or a foot of water, and to pull the boat by its painter, than it is to row against the wind. If you have to walk bent over and holding on to the bow, in order to pull the boat, your sacroiliac will probably snap out after the first hundred yards.

At blinds on small ponds or rivers, or narrow coves or inlets, a smaller boat will serve your purposes; but, even in these instances, I prefer a two-man boat–one man to row, one to shoot. Let us assume that you are alone in the boat and that you are chasing a cripple. When you get close enough to shoot, you have to pull on the oars thwartships and grope for your gun. This maneuver, in which the blades of the oars usually flash high in the air, particularly if you shove the handles under your knees, frequently frightens your quarry, and you will learn that even the dabbling river and pond ducks, such as the black and the mallard, can–if sufficiently frightened–swim under water like a U-boat. Thus, you will find yourself sitting in the boat, with your oars in the air, your gun in your hands and nothing to shoot at except ripples. The cripple may come up out of gunshot and you can enjoy the dubious pleasure of repeating the entire process all over again.

Thus the rule is:–

If the duck is merely crippled, let two men go–with two guns. If the duck is dead and the water not too rough, let one man go out in the boat. But be sure that the duck is dead. Take a glance at him through the glasses before you start. If his head is under water, the chances are that he is dead, or will be in a moment. If the head is still up, however, he may get up steam again and swim away. There will be more of this rule in the chapter called "Half an Hour Before Sunrise"; but I might add here that many, many times I have gone out alone in a boat to pick up what I thought was a dead duck, only to find that he had revived and could swim as fast, or faster, than I could row.

In pursuing a cripple with two men in a boat, remember to keep the duck on the port bow so the man in the stern can keep his eye on him. When you get near enough to shoot, one tug on the port oar, followed by a slight backwater on both oars, will check the progress of the boat and leave the cripple well to port. Then the man in the stern can get a comfortable and easier left shot without having to swing his gun across the center line of the boat. Never approach a cripple to your starboard unless, of course, you have aboard that comparative rarity, the left-handed gunner.

A few words should be said about the portable boat to be carried on the top of a car or on a trailer. If you want this boat for "a duck crawl," the smallest fiber-glass or plywood dinghy or "pumpkin seed" or the small aluminum boat will be the handiest one for you. Look out for it in bold water and realize that you have only a meager freeboard if you stuff the boat with two people.

It is better to carry the boat on the top of your car if you can manage it. Backing up with a trailer is difficult, and on rough ground is almost impossible. Further, the lanes which lead down to many gunning sites don't have nice paved "turn-arounds" at the end of them.

Since I have had practically no experience with collapsible boats or inflatable rubber boats, I really should not criticize them and shall not, outside of saying, first, that I view them with a more jaundiced emotion than suspicion; and, second, that it is one thing to be dumped into the pleasantly tepid water of midsummer when one is lightly dressed, and quite another to be dropped into water at just above thirty-two degrees when one is burdened with heavy gunning clothes and boots.

Precautions as to safety in the handling of guns should, of course, be observed at all times; but there are some special precautions which ought to be observed when guns and boats are mixed together.

Don't put a loaded gun in a boat and then drag the boat to the water. The gun, the muzzle of which is probably resting on the seat, while the heel of the stock is on the bottom of the boat, may be jolted off the seat to the floor. It might go off. Don't do this even with an unloaded gun. You might dent the barrel.

Now, the modern hammerless gun is a pretty safe affair, but it is not infallible any more than is mankind, who devised it.

Two friends of mine had two expensive English guns—the aggregate cost would have bought you a good new car and run it for a year or more. The guns were leaning thwartships in a boat on the shore. One man started to move the boat and one gun slid over sideways and hit the other. The sliding gun,

FIGURE 35 *Don't drag boat with guns in it. If one of these guns should go off there would be an additional listing in the obituary notices.*

presumably, went off first and destroyed the front six inches of one barrel of the other gun. The shock then set off both barrels of the other gun. Fortunately, no one was hurt. It taught me the lesson, however. Don't jolt a loaded gun.

So don't drag your boat with a loaded or unloaded gun in it. When the boat is afloat, put one gun, pointing aft with its barrel on the stern seat. The other may be placed pointing forward with its barrel on the bow seat, so that the barrel protrudes forward of the rower. If you are alone just lean it on the stern seat pointing aft.

Shooting from a boat is dangerous too. It is as if two gunners were sitting in a blind, facing each other. I think it is safer for only the passenger in the boat to shoot.

Of course, there are extenuating circumstances such as the time, years ago, when a gunning friend of mine and I rowed up on a flock of extra stupid bufflehead. We never thought that we would be able to approach them, but we came up closer than fifty yards and got six with the four barrels. But if you do it, be extra careful.

chapter five

THE GUN

The first principle as to what gun to use is: Shoot the gun which you can shoot the best and to which you are the most accustomed, even if it does not conform to some of the following suggestions, or to the advice of those better qualified to give it than I am.

Of course, I do not mean that you should try to hunt ducks with a .410 or a 28-gauge and, I think that I would also rule out the cylinder bore in any gauge unless the second barrel is a full or improved modified choke.

Guns fall roughly into five types:

(a) The single barrel
(b) The double barrel
(c) The pump
(d) The automatic
(e) The bolt action.

The single-barrel gun requires scant discussion. If it's all you have, shoot it. If you have anything else, at all suitable for duck hunting, shoot the anything else. The single-barrel shotgun is not adequate for this purpose. Too many crippled birds will get out of range before the gun can be reloaded.

A lot of single barrels have, and had, one safety feature which I was sorry to see leave practically all shotguns many, many years ago, namely, the hammer. This was usually of the rebounding type or of the half-cock safety type.

A similar hammer mechanism was also used on double-barrel guns from sometime after the invention of the percussion cap up until the turn of the century. I shot a double-barrel, side-hammer 10-gauge Parker until a few years ago. The hammer survived longest, however, in the single-barrel gun, in which it was usually placed in the center rather than at the side.

A glance at the hammer gun told you whether the gun was ready to go off or whether it was in a relatively inert condition. People got killed by carrying it loaded in a wagon or truck and by dragging it out, with the muzzle toward them, from under a lot of gear, so that the hammers fouled on something and, if the blocking mechanism failed, the gun went off. But you should not carry a loaded gun at any time in a vehicle.

Then there were the damn fools who carried these hammer guns cocked at all times. Actually, I suppose, the condition was not much more dangerous than that of the modern hammerless gun, which is always cocked but does not shout the warning at you by holding its ears back like an angry dog.

Yes, I know, a lot of people's thumbs slipped on the hammer, when letting it down from the full cocked position, and the gun went off. Well, they should have broken the gun before they let the hammers down, anyway. I made it an invariable rule with my old 10-gauge Parker.

But enough of this history. The hammer gun has joined the flintlock and the wheel lock in the mists of time, passed and gone.

The automatic and the pump give you three shots against the two of the double barrel. They used to give you five; but current federal regulations demand that a plug be placed in the magazines of these guns, so that they will hold but two shells in addition to the one in the chamber.

This third shot is, I must admit, an advantage when it comes to finishing off cripples while they are still in range, which they often are not by the time you have reloaded your double. However, I have observed that many hunters—particularly when armed with the automatic—feeling the assurance of the three shots at their disposal, let off the second shot too quickly or carelessly and thus reduce themselves to the humble level of their two-shot, double-barrel brethren, with the additional disadvantage that their third shots have to be let off at a greater range. Nevertheless, I must concede some advantage to the three-shell gun in this respect.

When it comes to rapidity of reloading, however, the double has the upper hand. Even without full ejectors—which I don't like anyway, first because I wear glasses and I don't care to have empty shells jumping up into my face and second because they usually make the gun stiff in opening—you can flip the empties out of a double and reload it before the automatic or pump man has got his second shell in the bottom of the gun.

Perhaps I should have admitted at the beginning of this chapter that I prefer the double gun. My older friends, with whom I shot at the now-dissolved Scarsdale Gun Club too many years ago to think about cheerfully, may be surprised at this statement because for twenty-five years I shot a Winchester pump model 12. This gun, in my opinion, is the finest pump gun ever made. In this quarter century of use—and it was fairly constant use because for nearly twenty years of that period the gun shot one to two hundred rounds a week—one firing pin broke and the catch on the breech block release wore out and had to be replaced. I imagine that the two repairs on the gun cost less than five dollars. I don't ever remember the gun jamming as so many pumps will. This is usually caused by the failure of the empty shell to eject, whereat the next loaded shell from the magazine fouls up with the empty inside the breech case. Then you have a task for a penknife or a screwdriver—but don't goose the primer on the live shell.

Someone in the back row asks, "Why did you change to a double gun?"

Well, to start off the change, an old friend of mine died and left me, in his will, the 10-gauge hammer Parker. I started to shoot it, first, perhaps because of sentiment; second, because the gun did fit me perfectly; third, because the dear old cannon held more powder and threw more lead and thus might improve my take-home pay in ducks.

In the last I was not disappointed.

I have, however, changed to a 12-gauge Parker, Vulcan grade, because the old 10-gauge had laminated steel barrels which are not safe for express loads, and sometimes, where I live, the lighter loads in this gauge were hard to come by.

After I had shot a double barrel for a while, I began to appreciate the real reasons for its superiority.

If, for example, you have overled or underled a duck and missed him with your first shot, the violent motion of working a pump-action gun, added to the recoil of the gun itself, tends to throw you off your target. With the double-barrel gun, however, the gun muzzle drops downward again after the recoil; you have, meanwhile, shifted your trigger finger to the rear trigger, and you find yourself on or near your target when you want to let off your second shot.

At this point I hear an automatic addict scrambling to his feet and declaring that the automatic gun offers these advantages and possesses two additional virtues in that you don't have to shift your finger and you have a third shot.

I'll concede the point, but. . . .

Perhaps I was born a little too early and that may engender in me the almost subconscious belief that the automatic is not entirely a sporting weapon. I hear howls of derision from the balcony, and I'll stipulate right now that this belief of mine is doubtless without foundation and erroneous. The automatic is a perfectly ethical gun; it may even create less cripples; it has less recoil, than the double or the pump—but my belief is unchanged. I know that it is probably wrong, but I just cannot argue myself out of it.

As to secondary reasons, the automatic is a fairly complex and delicate mechanism. Just get a little sand in the works, and you have to set up a field machine shop and take it all to pieces. Even then you cannot clean the inside of the breech properly. The same goes for the pump. The double has only three separable pieces from which you can blow or wipe the sand very easily.

Comes a very cold day, and the oil may get gummy on the tube over which the friction ring fits in the automatic. This ring controls the action of the bolt and if it does not operate properly, you have a jam; then the cold shivers run up and down my back, as I watch you probe with a knife or screwdriver into the viscera of the gun full of loaded shells.

A defective shell, or one outside of the tolerances established for shotgun shells, may cause a jam. If the discharged shell fails to eject from the chamber, shell number two, as in the pump, comes up on the carrier and the easiest thing to do—after the first ten minutes of struggle and profanity—is to get out of the blind, take off your gunning coat, spread it on a dry bit of ground —if there is any near—take the gun all to pieces and put the parts on the coat to keep the sand and dirt away from them.

Last but not the least of the objections to the automatic is the empty shell which is flung out with considerable force to the right of the gun. Unless the automatic gunner sits on the right side of the blind, he can be a nuisance to his companions.

The automatic is a fine lethal weapon when it works. When it doesn't, bluebills come into the stool.

The double-barrel gun has a few subspecies.

First, there is the over and under in which one barrel is placed above the other, instead of beside it, as in the more usual types. For the rifle shooter, who is accustomed to sighting along a single barrel and for the man who thinks that he gets astigmatism from looking along the converging barrels of a horizontal-type double gun, the over and under may have a definite appeal.

I suspect also that there is an element of snob appeal in the over and under. Until not too many years ago, the only over and unders I ever heard of were expensive foreign guns. This fact probably lends some glamour to the over and under, in spite of the fact that you can buy one today from Sears, Roebuck.

To my mind, there is one objection—and perhaps only one—to the over and under.

In order to load the lower barrel and extract the shell therefrom, it is necessary to design this gun so that it breaks open much farther than does the horizontal double-barrel type. This feature—or rather disadvantage—in my opinion, weakens the structure of the gun at the hinge point, where the stock and breech mechanism attach to the barrels. I have observed a variety of over and unders of domestic manufacture and many of them, after a great deal of use—and perhaps abuse—seem to develop looseness at the hinge.

One day, on a trap range, when closing a loaded over and under, made by a prominent American manufacturer, I had both barrels go off into the ground just as the thumb latch snapped into place. I had previously noticed that the mechanism of the gun was quite loose.

I have mentioned full ejectors before. This type of gun throws the empty shells out when the gun is broken open. To my previous objections to this type—namely that they endanger one's eyeglasses and render the gun very stiff to open, inasmuch as you must compress the two powerful ejector springs when you perform this operation—I might add that, in a gunning blind the full ejector can be most annoying to your companions.

Perhaps you have just fired your two shots and there is a cripple out front trying to get away. Your fellow gunner is just drawing a bead on the flapping cripple, when you open your gun and the blind seems to be filled with flying bouncing empty shells. There are only two, of course, but there appear to be six. This performance creates a disagreeable distraction, and I have seen many a duck get away because of it.

The full ejector is a pleasant—albeit unnecessary—gadget in a field gun. In a blind, it borders on the discourteous.

The single selective trigger appears usually on the more expensive models of foreign-made guns. This device permits one to shoot first one barrel and then the other by pulling the single trigger twice. There is usually in addition a selector lever or button by means of which you can choose which barrel will be fired first.

In effect this feature makes the double-barrel gun a two-shot automatic. The main drawback to this feature is that you cannot select your full choke barrel without first fumbling with the selector lever. In the two-trigger gun you merely pull the trigger you want.

It is, in some respects, a handy and efficient but expensive feature and, I might add, that many of those which I have seen break down and have to be sent to the gun hospital every few years. In my opinion, it is too delicate a mechanism to be reliable. Worse yet, it usually goes out of order at a crucial moment and when it does, either both barrels go off upon one pull of the trigger or the gun won't discharge at all.

Before we pass on to gauges and chokes, I suppose I should mention briefly that miscegenetic contraption–the bolt-action shotgun. It is a perfectly good, reliable gun so far as strength of breech and dependability of loading mechanism is concerned. The bolt action breech is extremely strong and simple and is easy to clean and service. That is probably why it is employed on most high-power rifles and, I believe, all military rifles. Its application to a shotgun was, however, in my opinion, an error. I don't believe that the bolt-action gun is really much better than the single shot for duck hunting.

In order to put your second shell in the chamber, you have to take your hand off the trigger guard and the small of the stock, fumble for the bolt handle, which probably lies outside the cone of your vision, move your head back or to one side so that you won't put your eye out with the bolt when you pull it back, snap back the bolt smartly so as to eject the empty shell cleanly, and slam it forward again to push the second shell into the chamber.

Neither the second duck nor the cripple is going to delay his departure while you go through all these operations and then get your cheek down on the stock again.

GADGETS FOR GUNS

I don't want to offend the manufacturers of gadgets for shotguns, but I do not know of one which I consider essential to duck hunting except the rubber butt pad, and even this—inasmuch as the duck hunter is pretty well insulated with a lot of clothes—serves more to lengthen the stock of his gun than to protect him from recoil. There will be more about length of stock and drop at the heel in the chapter on Shooting the Gun; but I do want to mention that I believe that the recoil of a 12-gauge gun is often overemphasized by a lot of people. Of course, I weigh about two hundred pounds without my gunning clothes; since that is a lot of hamburger for a gun to push around, I don't even notice the recoil. Anyone weighing over a hundred and thirty pounds who holds his gun correctly and whose gun fits him passing well, does not need a butt pad for duck hunting. If he plans to burn up a few hundred shells at trap shooting, that is an entirely different thing—even with the light trap loads.

Personally, I use a rubber butt pad—not for the protection of my carcass, but because my gun, when I bought it, was too short for me.

The butt pad is better when it gets old and a little crystallized. When it is new, its coefficient of friction is very high, and it is apt to catch on your clothes when you bring gun to shoulder. Rub a little talcum powder into the end of the pad if you have this trouble; it will help a lot.

FIGURE 36 *A good butt pad. Holes lend it plenty of resiliency.*

There are several shotgun sights on the market, some of which are of the concentric-ring type. The general idea of these is that you can tell the range of the duck by the amount of space he occupies in the sight, and by solving a trigonometry problem in your head as the duck flies over the stool, you determine whether to lead him by one ring or two.

Some people may be able to use these to good advantage, but frankly, I cannot. Perhaps I learned my bad habits in gunning too long ago to be able to rectify them now. I find these sights confusing and the type in which one looks through a darkened glass is apt to get blurred on rainy or foggy days. They might, however, be useful to a man who is just learning to shoot.

We shall deal with the question of swing and lead in a later chapter. Here I shall point out only that I find these sights very confusing, particularly on incoming and going away shots.

Quite a few people use variable chokes on their guns. Of course, these can be attached only to the single-barrel gun—single shot, pump, bolt action, or automatic. By means of this device, different degrees of choke may be established in your gun.*

I can appreciate that, if you use the same gun for duck shooting, for upland shooting, for traps and for skeet, such a device might have considerable utility; but inasmuch as I confine my gunning activities to ducks, I don't find much use for it. Surely you are not going to take the time to open your variable choke because a duck lands in the water between you and the stool; nor are you going to turn it up to full choke for a passing shot at a duck twenty yards the other side of the stool. If you do, you might as well go on a bird walk and leave your gun at home.

The compensator comprises a tube about five inches long, which again can be attached only to single-barrel guns. It has slots cut through its surface into the extension of the barrel and

* For the very few who do not know, choke is a constriction of the bore in the last few inches at the muzzle for the purpose of packing the shot string together, thus obtaining a closer pattern.

these are arranged in such a way that the blast of gases bears forward against them and thus the recoil is reduced. Some types of compensators come with a set of three or four different chokes, which, by means of a wrench, can be attached to the forward end of the compensator.

The compensator does reduce the recoil to some extent, although, as I have said before, I do not think that recoil in gunning clothes is an important factor if your gun fits you properly.

As to the different chokes available with this device, my comments on the variable choke apply, except, of course, that the variable choke can be changed comparatively quickly by turning a knurled sleeve and, in the compensator type, the undesired choke has to be taken off with the wrench and the desired one screwed on—also with the wrench. Again, this device may have considerable utility if you use your gun for upland shooting and skeet as well as for duck hunting.

OLD GUNS

Some mention should be made of the dangers which lurk in old guns.

The Damascus or twist barrel can readily be identified. These barrels, instead of being smooth as is the modern barrel, appear to have been constructed of spirally twisted wires, welded together. As a matter of fact, that is how they were made. Other similar-type barrels are covered with little swirls of metal which lend them a most attractive and decorative appearance.

All of these guns, however, are booby traps.

The Damascus or twist barrels were designed to withstand the lower pressures of black powder *and should never be used with any other kind.*

Even the comparatively low-pressure powder, known as bulk smokeless, should not be used in these guns. Radical temperature changes can sometimes alter the pressures delivered by such powders.

I know that a lot of people have an Uncle Hiram, who always shoots "Super X" express shells in his old twist-barrel gun.

Just wait. Someday Uncle Hiram will lose an eye or two and most of the fingers of his left hand.

I have seen these barrels turned inside out for a couple of feet of their length. The effect is pretty nearly as bad as holding a hand grenade while it goes off.

There is another type of barrel which was made, here and abroad, at about the turn of the century. This one can fool you easily because it looks exactly like a modern fluid-steel barrel. This is the so-called laminated steel barrel.

It was made to shoot bulk smokeless and the other low-pressure powders of its day and can be used with safety with the modern low-pressure loads; but *never* put an express shell in it. You may not live to regret it.

GAUGE AND CHOKE

Back in the boisterous nineteenth century, 8-gauge guns and even 4-gauge guns were made and used. As far as I know, they all were designed to employ black powder.

Now, of course, the federal law prohibits the use of bores larger than the 10-gauge in the taking of migratory water fowl.

I have an affection for the 10-gauge. It has a hearty satisfying bellow when it goes off; and if your right hand is frozen solid so that it cannot feel the triggers, and if your numbed forefinger thus slips off the front trigger and sets off the rear one too, the old gun will sit you down in the blind as quickly and as efficaciously as the thrust from the hind hoof of a mule.

But it is not too practical a gun today.

As far as I can find out, none are made any more in this country by the large manufacturers, and most of those made in the past were not constructed with fluid-steel barrels. I understand that now some of the Belgian gun makers will fit high-pressure 10-gauge barrels in the place of the old ones at a not too great cost. However, the ammunition is becoming increasingly difficult to obtain in out-of-the-way places.

From the emotional point of view, it is a lovely gun—but I would not buy one.

The 12-gauge gun is really the most satisfactory for ducks. A reference to the shot table on page 75 will prove that it is not much inferior to the 10-gauge and considerably better from that point of view than the 16- or 20-gauges. In fact, the 10-gauge in the light 1¼-oz. load, which should be used with the majority of those guns, carries the same number of shot as the 12-gauge express load.

The thirty-inch barrel gives you a little more range, and at the same time does not make the gun so cumbersome that you have to put wheels on it for upland shooting.

Speaking of upland shooting, if you do, or plan to do, a great deal of it in addition to duck hunting, you can use the 16-gauge for both. However, I really doubt that it is worth while to drop to the 16-gauge. The only reason for doing it would be to save yourself the burden of carrying the heaviest hardware around. I note that the current Winchester double-barrel weighs the same in 16-gauge as it does in 12-gauge.*

20-gauge,* in my opinion, is definitely too small for ducks, although I must admit that I have seen experts do some wonderful duck shooting with this lady's gun.

As to choke, if you plan to buy a single-barrel gun—automatic or pump—by all means get it in full choke for duck hunting. The humanitarian aspects of finishing off cripples is sufficient reason without giving others.

If you plan to buy a double-barrel gun, I like the modified or the improved modified choke for the right barrel and full choke for the left. Thus you obtain a larger pattern for your first and usually closer shot and the carrying power and denser pattern for your second and usually longer shot.

Most everyone, of course, is familiar with what *choke* is; but it might be worth while to mention for the benefit of the more curious just what its effects are and how it is measured.

The full-choke gun when fired at the center of a thirty-inch circle at a range of forty yards is supposed to place about

* See Table on page 75 for comparison of shot charges.

70 per cent of its pellets within the circle. The improved modified is supposed to register a score of around 60 per cent, the modified about 50 per cent, the improved cylinder substantially 40 per cent and the cylinder about 30 per cent.

If you cannot get a new dime into the muzzle of your 12-gauge gun, it is full choke.* If you can, it is a modified choke, or larger than that.

Now, to emphasize the importance of choke, let's put up an imaginary duck on the wing at this same forty-yard distance. Let us also say that he offers a going away shot because, if he were coming toward you, you would wait until he came closer.

FIGURE 37 *Shells – left to right 10 gauge, 12 gauge, 16 gauge, 20 gauge and .410.*

FIGURE 38 *The same – showing shell heads.*

* The actual bore—not the choke—of a 12-gauge gun is .729 inch. The term 12-gauge comes down from the old days and means that 12 balls which just fit the bore of this gun will, together, weigh 1 pound. Thus, the larger the gauge number the smaller the bore.

Assume for the purposes of this demonstration that he offers a target area of twenty-five square inches—that he is a small duck such as a teal or a bufflehead. That is not counting his feathers, of course; just his carcass and wings. Assume also a 12-gauge gun and 1¼ ounces of 4 shot. There are, as the table on this page shows, 169 shot in this load of which, with a full-choke gun, 118 will theoretically be within the 30-inch circle at this range. But the duck's target area is only 1/28 of the area of the circle, so by application of the quantum theory and the laws of probabilities, only 4 pellets should strike him, assuming further—and erroneously, of course—that the pattern is regular. With the modified bore there would be 3 pellets in his target area, and with the cylinder bore, less than two pellets.

Number of Shot Pellets in 1⅝-oz. Load for 10-Gauge Shell*

Size of Shot	7½	6	5	4	2
Number of Shot	568	365	275	220	145

Number of Shot Pellets in 1¼-oz. Load for 12-Gauge Shell*

Size of Shot	7½	6	5	4	2
Number of Shot	437	281	212	169	112

Number of Shot Pellets in 1⅛-oz. Load for 16-Gauge Shell*

Size of Shot	7½	6	5	4	2
Number of Shot	394	253	191	152	101

Number of Shot Pellets in 1-oz. Load for 20-Gauge Shell*

Size of Shot	7½	6	5	4	2
Number of Shot	350	225	170	135	90

* Data furnished by Western Cartridge Company, Division of Olin Industries, Inc., East Alton, Illinois.

Look at the problem in another way for a moment, and assume again (and again erroneously) regularity of pattern. How many square inches does each of these pellets occupy alone within the hypothetical 30-inch circle? In other words, what is the density of the pattern?

With the full choke it is 6 square inches; with the modified, nearly 9 square inches; with the cylinder, about 14 square inches.

Now remove the erroneous assumption of regularity of pattern and admit that we may have gaps in it through which a duck may pass unscathed at not much beyond forty yards, and you can readily see the all-important need of the full choke to keep the pellets as concentrated as possible.

Speaking of patterns, I think it is a good idea to pattern your own gun; but I want to warn you before you start that to do so takes patience, perseverance and quite a lot of shells.

The value of running patterns on your gun is that, for reasons which no one has ever been able to explain to me, two guns of the same make, model, choke and vintage will make different patterns with the same size of shot and measure of powder. Often a gun will make better patterns with a lighter load than it will with an express load. But let's not get into that, unless you want to, for you will have so many variables that you may get nowhere. So try first the express loads which you will employ for duck hunting.

Buy about four dozen 30-inch-circle pattern targets from your gun shop. A double-spread sheet of newspaper will do, although it really is not quite big enough, being but 23″ x 32″. If you feel economical and use newspapers, put big bull's-eyes in the centers with black paint.

If you do not plan to use the gun for upland shooting, it will be enough, perhaps, to test four sizes of shot: 7½'s, 6's, 5's and 4's. If you are going upland shooting, test 8's and perhaps 9's also. I would forget about the 2's. You will employ them only for distant cripples or for geese.

I suppose that to pattern a gun properly one should fire from fifty to one hundred shells of each size of shot and, with an adding machine, average the whole lot. However, this would represent about a week's hard work of trudging back and forth to change the target. So let's take ten shells of each size of shot. Even this is going to be a three-hour job.

Shoot from a rest, so as to eliminate as much of the human error as possible; mark each target with the number of size of shot used, and number your targets one to ten. Run the test on a windless day, if possible, and don't under any circumstances try to pattern in a cross wind.

With a double-barrel gun, you probably should run ten shots for each barrel; but try five first and see how much variation you get.

In counting the shot holes in the target, mark them with a ballpoint pen. I put a circle around each tenth hole and mark it, 1 for 10, 2 for twenty, etc. This will help you not to lose count. Gaps in the patterns should be taken into consideration as well as the number of shot holes in the circle. These gaps will demonstrate to you why you miss a duck completely when you are sure you are on him and have him cold.

After you have taken all this trouble to make your calculations, by all means be guided by what you find. If your right barrel makes more satisfactory patterns with 7½'s than it does with 6's, use the 7½'s in your right barrel. If 6's or 5's make a better showing in your left barrel than 4's, use the best size. If you have any doubts, run some of the tests over again.

If your tests show that your gun shoots all sizes about as it should, according to the above figures, with a variation of only about 5 per cent, plus or minus, calculated upon the total number of pellets in the load, then you are lucky, and I would recommend 6's and 4's as pointed out in the next section.

Of course, there is one drawback to owning a gun that shoots a good clean pattern with no bad gaps. If you miss a duck you can't blame it on the gun; you will have to shoulder the responsibility yourself.

In reading the following section on Ammunition, bear in mind that the recommendations made therein should be adjusted to the results of any pattern tests which you may make on your gun.

AMMUNITION

A glance at the table on page 75 will give you a good idea of the number of pellets in shells in various loads and gauges.

Up to perhaps forty-odd yards it may be assumed that the smaller the shot (i.e., the larger the size number of the shot) the denser the pattern made by it will be and thus the smaller the gaps between the pellets. Beyond that, the lighter shot, being the more easily affected by air resistance, drops off rapidly in its velocity and thus in its killing power.

That, however, is not the whole story. Like almost everything else in life, the question of the size of shot is a compromise with the ideal.

If we compare the shocking power of a 7½ pellet to that of a 4 pellet (assuming their velocities to be the same, an assumption which increases in error with the range) we find that it would take about three 7½ pellets to equal the shocking power of one 4. Compared with a 2, we find that it would take about four 7½'s to equal the shocking power of a 2.*

I know a few people who use 7½'s exclusively in duck hunting and obtain good results. With the decoys set close into the blind, you do get a beautiful pattern with the 7½'s. However, if you are going to use this size of shot, a selection which I don't recommend, except perhaps for the right barrel, you will have to use self-control and pass up those long shots which are so tempting; otherwise, you will have the unhappy feeling at the end of the shoot that you have caused a thoughtlessly unnecessary number of cripples.

I prefer and use the heavier shot and usually place 6's in the right barrel and 4's in the left, for the second and usually the longer shot. I also always keep in my cartridge belt, in the

* To satisfy those with a healthy and well-developed sense of curiosity, the striking energy of one 2 shot at forty yards, fired from an express shell, is about 8.5 foot pounds. The effect of this on a two- or three-pound duck is about the same as that produced on an average-sized man by the impact of a heavy-caliber revolver bullet.

extreme right set of loops, three or four shells loaded with 2 shot. These are used for cripples at long range and are also kept on hand in the hope that a goose may come along.

The 5 shot was a good compromise between 4's and 6's, and I used them for years. Having but one size in my belt—except for the few 2's—was a great convenience because I did not have to puzzle out the numbers on the ends of the shells each time I reloaded. The 5's are often hard to get now, so I employ the 6's and the 4's, also the 6's do give a better pattern.

Speaking of puzzling out the numbers on shells, I would like to digress here a moment with a combination gripe against and suggestion to the shell manufactuers.

It would be fine to be able to tell the shot size by a quick glance at the shell.

At the present time, each manufacturer uses a different colored paper for his shells. A few of them use substantially the same color. But every manufacturer places all sizes of shot in the same color shells.

Years ago, you had to get out your pocket magnifying glass to read the minute numbers which were printed dimly on the shot wad, in 4-point type, to tell you the load and the size of the shot.

Then some manufacturers brought out the flat-ended shell, which incidentally gives a far better pattern than the old type, and on this new surface they pasted a disc of paper with a good large legible number in perhaps 14-point type. This helped a lot, except that, come a spell of damp weather, many of the discs fell off and then you had no idea as to whether you were putting 7½'s in your gun or 2's.

Recently they started printing the number of the size of shot in smudgy semi-disappearing ink on the side of the shell. The number is all mixed up with a lot of semilegible trademarks and the name of the manufacturer and the whole arrangement puts me in mind of those confused multilined drawings, so popular in children's magazines, forty years ago, which you had to turn upside down or sideways in order to make out the cat or the pig or what have you hidden in the picture.

Now, why in the dickens don't all the shell manufacturers get together—yes, and let the Department of Justice attend the meeting, too, so that it can see that there is nothing dirty going on. Why, at such a meeting, couldn't the manufacturers agree on a different colored shell for each size of shot and then all of them adhere to that color system? Of course, they would still have to print the size number of the shot, too, for the benefit of those who are color-blind. For example, suppose they could agree on the following:

Size of Shot	Color of Shell
9	black
8	orange
7½	red
6	yellow
5	gray
4	blue
2	white
BB	green
00	brown
single ball	pink
rifled slug	purple

"But," say the manufacturers of shells, "it would be too expensive to keep and handle a different color of paper stock—ten different colors or more—for the various sizes of shot."

My answer to that would be that, if that is so, they could adopt the next best method.

At the present time the manufacturers print on the sides of their shells—I assume after they are loaded. Why couldn't they print a wide band of color—assuming the stock to be of some dull neutral tone—so that the band would stand out clearly?

Such a step would be a real convenience to the duck hunter, and there are about two million of them in the country now. I'll wager that the manufacturer who first adopts this system will increase his sales vastly.

EXPRESS LOADS OR STANDARD LOADS

As mentioned above, the shell manufacturers used to mark three items of information on each shell, the dram equivalent, in black powder, of the charge; the weight of the load of shot in ounces; the size of the shot. Nowadays they put only the shot size on the shell. The full information appears only on the box, and in some cases not even there.

The so-called express or high-velocity load for the 12-gauge shell is usually:

3 ¾ drams equivalent of powder
1 ¼ ounces of shot

The low-pressure or standard load is usually:

3 drams equivalent of powder
1 ⅛ ounces of shot.

Thus the express load has 25 per cent more powder than the standard load; but, inasmuch as the express load has to push only 11 per cent more in weight of shot than does the standard load, it throws this pro rata lighter load at a higher velocity. The express, probably, has a somewhat greater range, too.

Most twelve-gauge guns—except some of the foreign-made light-weight field guns for upland work, which have shorter chambers—are chambered for the 2 ¾-inch shell. I have shot, but not owned, the twelve-gauge chambered for the 3-inch, so-called magnum shell. This, of course, is a magnificent shell for duck shooting. It throws the same weight of shot at the standard 2 ⅞-inch 10-gauge shell, namely 1 ⅝ oz., and has excellent killing power at long range.

If you plan to use your gun only for duck hunting, you will doubtless be pleased with the 3-inch magnum, but if you plan to use it for upland shooting too, you will find it pretty heavy to drag about on a long day's tramp. There is one other drawback to this gun, even if it is to be employed solely for duck hunting. In out-of-the-way places, it is difficult and often impossible to purchase the 3-inch magnum shell, and I have it on good authority that the 2 ¾-inch shell in a 3-inch chamber will not make a good pattern. I do not know the reason for this, but it may be that due to the fact that since the shell is too short for the chamber, the shot may become marred and distorted by the ridge located at the point where the chamber ends and the barrel begins.

I have never tried the 2¾-inch shell in a 3-inch pump gun, but I can imagine that it might give trouble in the feeding mechanism. I have not seen an automatic shotgun chambered for the 3-inch shell.

Therefore, attractive as the 3-inch magnum is—and I have always wanted to own one—I think that, if you plan to possess but one gun, you will do better with the 2¾-inch chamber.

To sum up the brief dissertation on ammunition, I think that it is better to use the express shells for ducks. The higher velocity gives, of course, a greater shocking power to the pellets which actually hit the duck*; but, more important than that, they give you a somewhat greater killing range. An extra five yards of killing range often makes the difference between finishing off an unfortunate cripple and losing him so that he swims away, perhaps to serve later as luncheon for the gulls and crows.

CARE OF THE GUN

Back in the good old days of the fulminate of mercury primer, one cleaned one's gun right after the shoot—or should have. The salts deposited in the barrel by this type of primer—which had been but little improved since its invention by Forsythe, early in the nineteenth century—were, as I understand it, corrosive in themselves and were extremely hydroscopic. Thus, lack of proper cleaning could and did result in both corrosion and rust.

Since the development of the noncorrosive primer, a few decades ago, all this is changed. It is, of course, a good idea to clean your gun before you put it away for any length of time, and if you are shooting for several days in succession, it is advisable to run an oily rag, or one soaked in "Hoppe's Powder Solvent, No. 9" through the barrel to be sure that you are not getting any leading in your barrel. Soft shot is not used any more. All modern loads employ chilled shot, which is harder and much

* About 25 per cent more at forty yards.

less likely to mark up and stick to the barrel. However, in spite of the chilled shot, this sometimes does happen. The cure is a liberal application of Hoppe's followed by the judicious use of a wire brush soaked in the same preparation.

If this won't remove the lead, take your gun to a gunsmith. Don't try to scrape it out with the sharp edge of a metal curtain rod or similar implement. You will only scratch your barrel, and it will lead up again more quickly than ever. For the same reason, always use a wooden cleaning rod, never a metal one.

It is preferable, too, to clean a gun from the breech end. The threaded metal ferrules, by means of which the sections of your cleaning rod are fastened together, should be made of brass, but sometimes they are not. Even brass, although it is much softer than steel, could mar the all-important muzzle of your gun,

FIGURE 39 *Jointed wooden cleaning rod with wire brush of brass bristles.*

should you introduce the cleaning rod at that end. Marring of the muzzle and choke will give you an erratic and unreliable pattern.

Perhaps it is not necessary to suggest this, but, if you shoot in the rain, you should disassemble your gun as soon as you get under cover. Wipe it first with a dry rag with no oil on it, for the oil and water drops will form an emulsion which may, subsequently, rust the gun. Then go over it with a well-oiled rag. Give the same treatment to the inside of the barrel, in which some rain drops may be lurking.

The double barrel is, naturally, much easier to clean than the pump or the automatic, although the rain water tends to creep down on the face of the breech block and may seep into the lock mechanism through the firing pin holes. There is nothing much that you can do about this in a gun with nondemountable locks, except to wipe off the water and force oil into the firing-pin holes and up into the locks through the slots through which the triggers come out. It is not a good idea to demount and remount nondemountable locks frequently, unless you possess a set of gunsmith's screwdrivers and are a scrupulously careful mechanic.

Rain also gets under the forearm. Be sure that you wipe dry all the wood and metal parts.

Rain on the pump gun and the automatic presents greater problems in cleaning; but the principles are the same. One friend of mine who took great pride in his Browning automatic—an imported one—used to stand it muzzle down in an open-topped drum of fuel oil. This treatment appears to be quite radical; but evidently it is good, for the gun, which is twenty years old, looks brand-new today.

By all means have a case for your gun.

The leg-o'-mutton cases and their less expensive relatives, the double-section canvas cases, which involve taking down the gun before inserting it, are all right for storage and are handy for traveling. They are, however, a nuisance to take out to a blind, or on a duck crawl from pothole to pothole, when you will be dragging your gun in and out of a car or truck. It's a lot of trouble, on a cold December morning, to have to disassemble a gun when your hands are about as facile as a pair of flounders just removed from the deep freeze.

If you are proud of your gun, you don't want to carry it about without a case and let it bang against other guns in the back seat of the car or in the body of the truck. So, unless you do the kind of hunting where you can shoot ducks from your bedroom window, buy a full-length case, so that your gun is ready for use as soon as you take it from the case.

The best case which I have seen for this purpose is the one made of sheepskin, with the wool turned in. The wool gradually absorbs oil from the gun and preserves it. The thickness of the case also protects the gun from scratches and dents. Its only weakness is that it is not waterproof.

FIGURE 40 *The sheepskin guncase. This protects gun which can be carried assembled.*

When the season is over, and a gun is to be put away for several months, many people coat it inside and out with a heavy gun grease or motor oil of about a 30 S.A.E. viscosity.

I believe that this is unnecessary, and I am sure that you will regret it when you take the gun out again next year and start digging the grease or coagulated oil off it. If you use a good grade of fairly high viscosity oil such as NYOIL, apply it liberally, put your gun in a case and store it in a dry place–no cellars please–it will be ready for use next autumn when the leaves begin to fall.

chapter six

SHOOTING THE GUN

Among all the sins of commission and of omission in shotgun shooting, the most common, persistent and disheartening error is that of *seeing the barrel.*

This habit makes you shoot way high, and you'll probably shoot over your duck every time.

Shotgun shooting differs greatly from rifle shooting. The latter is generally a static action, while shooting a shotgun is dynamic. With the rifle you hold as closely and as steadily as possible on the game or target, and then squeeze the trigger carefully so as to avoid disturbing your aim. In the case of the shotgun, the target or game is almost always moving, and the technique of shooting is entirely different.

Take your gun and go out of doors, wearing about the same weight of clothes you would have on in a gunning blind. Stand with the left foot well—but not awkwardly—ahead of the right. Bring the empty gun smartly to your shoulder, drop your cheek lightly but firmly to the comb of the stock and sight along the barrel. You can close the left eye, or leave both eyes open, whichever is easier for you. More on this subject later.

What do you see of the gun?

What you should see is the bead sight of the muzzle standing upon the groove of the breech. You should see only the bead and *no part* of the intervening barrel between the breech and the bead. Be sure that you see all of the bead, else you will shoot low.

If you do see any of the barrel—and, of course, it will appear at the muzzle end—then the gun does not fit you.

One of two things may be wrong:

(a) The stock may be too short for you
(b) It may have insufficient drop,* i.e., the stock may be too straight with reference to the barrel.

To cure this, first try to lengthen the stock. You can accomplish this, at least on a temporary and test basis, by buying a cheap stock boot—the kind that fits over the heel and toe and laces up forward of the toe. Cut up some thick cardboard in the shape of the inside of the sole of the boot. Make six or eight of these inner soles and try the gun on again for size. If you still see barrel, after adding an inch to an inch and a half to the length of the stock, or if you have to grind your cheekbone into the stock to avoid seeing it, you will have to have the drop in your gun increased. This is a job for a gunsmith.

Many gunsmiths have adjustable stocks for fitting purposes and if you go to one of them, he can tell you how much drop you should have.

Incidentally, if you have to shove your cheek down hard against the stock in order to avoid seeing barrel, you will develop a most tender and sensitive mouse on your cheek from the recoil of the gun. This will hurt you each time the gun goes off, and the hurt will result in a flinch or an unconscious lifting of the

* Drop at heel of stock is the distance between the heel of the stock and the rearward continuation of the line of the barrels. You can measure it fairly closely by putting the gun upside down on a table with the front sight over the edge and measuring the height of the tip of the heel of the stock above the table. "Drop" should not be confused with "pitch," which relates to the angle made between the line of the butt plate and the line of the barrel. To measure it, stand the gun with the butt plate flat on the floor with the top rear of the breech just touching the wall. The distance from the wall to the muzzle of the gun is the pitch.

head just before the trigger is pulled. Either can ruin your shooting.

Before you go to a gunsmith, however, try the lengthening process, because lengthening the gun also increases the drop a little. Put the gun upside down on the table again, and you'll see what I mean.

An ill-fitting gun, however, is not the only cause for seeing barrel.

Curiosity, lack of self-control, or lack of concentration —whichever you want to select—produces this sin perhaps even more frequently than the misfit gun.

When you put your cheek down on the stock and see only the muzzle sight over the breech—*and no barrel*—try to imagine that the gun has become an integral and unjoined part of your head, shoulders and arms. As you swing the gun, from side to side and up and down, your view of the gun should not change one iota. Pointing in any direction you should see only the muzzle sight nestling in the breech groove—AND NO BARREL.

Now this is easy to do in the back yard. You can swing your gun on the chimney and on the top of the clothes dryer, and never see any barrel. But now let us look at what you will do in a duck blind, if you are not careful.

It is a very tempting thing to do to lift your head, particularly on an incoming shot or on a crossing shot where the duck is flying from your left to your right.

If you fire correctly at a duck coming straight in to you, you should lift the gun along his line of flight, catch up to him, pass him (i.e., aim above him so that the muzzle of the gun conceals him from your view). Then you pull the trigger. It is just before you pull the trigger that the temptation comes. The duck is obscured by the gun. You think that maybe you are overleading him. You lift your head to take a peek. Lifting an inch will ruin the shot. Sure, the duck is still there; but now that you see him you are inclined to give him more lead. You do. Bang! You've missed him and overled him perhaps by three or four feet.

On the crossing shot from your left to right, there is a somewhat similar condition. If, as I did, you started rifle shooting years before you began shotgun shooting, you will probably find it difficult to deny the almost reflex action of closing the left eye as soon as you lift the gun to your shoulder. In twenty-odd years of trapshooting, I tried in vain to train myself to shoot with both eyes open. Thus, I have come to the conclusion that, if keeping both eyes open makes you feel cross-eyed, you might as well relax and close the left eye. However, shooting with both eyes open gives you binocular vision, with the attendant advantage of being able to judge distance better, and it is an ability well worth trying to acquire. Practice it first with clay birds and the trap, before you waste any shots at ducks.

Let us say that you *do* shoot with the left eye closed.

When the head is down on the stock, it is inclined slightly to the right and, with the left eye closed, your vision beyond a few degrees to the left of the gun is blocked.

You follow this left-to-right-flying duck with your gun, catch up to him with your sights, pass him and then lead him. At this point he gets near the periphery of the field of vision of your right eye, and again there comes that perfectly natural, reflex temptation to lift your head in order to see him more clearly.

Don't give in. If you do, you're sure to shoot over him.

Like most evils, this one of seeing barrel has a converse. A gun with too much drop will not permit you to see the muzzle bead if your cheek is snugly against the comb. You will have to lift your head in order to achieve your line of sight and to avoid shooting low. If your cheek is not firmly against the stock, then the relationship of your eye and the gun is not fixed and rigid, as it should be, you and the gun will be adrift from each other and the gun will not be an integral part of your arms, head and shoulders, as it must be in order for you to shoot well.

This converse evil may be cured by a comb pad to raise the head slightly. Having a gunsmith effect a decrease in the drop of the gun will probably result in a better and more permanent correction.

Some gunners, in leading a duck, do not swing their guns with the duck's line of flight. Instead, they aim at a spot in the air ahead of the duck, and when they estimate that the duck is about the right distance from this spot, they pull the trigger. Some people do quite well with this kind of snap shooting; but I truly think that the swinging lead is better and more reliable—particularly if the duck deviates from a straight line in his flight.

Now, I suppose that the concept of swinging the gun with the line of flight of the duck arose in those centuries in which the flintlock was the standard form of ignition. I have shot many flintlocks and can say that the first thing which is difficult to get accustomed to is the comparatively long delay between the time the trigger is pulled and the time at which the piece goes off. It varies a great deal with the dryness and fineness of the priming powder, and on a damp day it must run to a second. Therefore, the gunner of that time with his "fowling piece" never knew exactly when his gun would go off after he pulled the trigger; thus he had to swing with the bird, attain what he judged to be the proper lead, pull the trigger and keep on with the swing at the same pace, while the flint struck the frizzen, the sparks fell upon the priming powder, the priming powder was ignited and the blast of fire finally went through the touch-hole and ignited the main charge.

I think that this is the way to shoot today. There is a rhythm to it and a natural synchronism with the flight of the duck which, I have found, give better results than snap shooting. Lastly, remember that it takes you nearly ⅕th of a second to pull the trigger, after you make up your mind to do it. Thus, if you maintain your swing, you will retain your lead.

LEADING

It is with considerable trepidation that I approach this highly controversial subject of leading. A great deal has been written about it by a lot of people who are more competent to discuss the question than I am; but, like the man who is called upon to make an after-dinner speech, I must say a few words. Unlike most such men, I really mean *a few.*

Three elements enter into the question of leading:

(1) The speed of the charge
(2) The speed of the duck
(3) The distance from the gun to the duck

FIGURE 41 *Fair shooting stance.*

FIGURE 42 *Better shooting stance. Forward cant of body absorbs recoil better and preserves balance for a quick second shot.*

Of these three, we know, with any degree of accuracy, only the first. The muzzle velocity of the express shell is about 1,300 to 1,400 feet per second. Its integrated speed over a distance of 40 yards might be somewhere in the neighborhood of 1,000 feet per second depending on the size of the shot.

As to (2): A duck who is not in too great a hurry might —if he is crossing the stool and not planning to make a stop there —travel at thirty to thirty-five miles an hour. But how do you know? He might be interested in the stool and be doing only twenty. He might be frightened and doing fifty.

As to (3): How far away is he? If he's a big black at forty yards, you might guess that he is twenty-five yards away. If he is a little teal, at twenty-five yards, you might guess him to be at forty yards.

Let's take the above brackets of figures and, by means of a little sixth-grade arithmetic, determine what the theoretical lead should be at both ends of both brackets. For the purpose of this calculation, we shall pretend that there is no wind today and that the duck is flying at substantially 90 degrees to your line of fire. I shall deal with the question of wind a little further on.

We shall also assume an integrated rate for the shot charge of 1,000 ft. per second for the distances of twenty-five and forty yards. This, of course, is not quite accurate, but it is close enough for our purposes.*

The charge from the express shell will take .075 seconds to travel 25 yards. It will take .12 seconds to travel 40 yards.†

The duck at thirty-five miles per hour is covering 51 feet per second, and at twenty miles per hour, he is putting behind him 29 feet each second.

* For example 4 shot takes about .05 seconds to travel 20 yards. However, to travel 60 yards, or three times that distance, it takes four times that long or about .2 seconds.
† It should be recognized that the heavier shot maintains its velocity somewhat better than the lighter shot upon which air resistance has a greater effect. For instance, 7½ shot takes .23 seconds to travel sixty yards while 4 shot covers the same distance in .2 seconds. The rifled slug would take .14 seconds. For the purposes of this broad discussion, this and other minor factors will be ignored.

At the thirty-five-mile-per-hour speed, he will—if he is twenty-five yards away from the gun—cover about four feet between the time the trigger is pulled and the time the charge reaches him. At the forty-yard distance, and at the same speed, he will cover about 6.1 feet in the same interval.

At the twenty-miles-per-hour speed, he will, at twenty-five yards from the gun, move 2.1 feet in the interval between trigger pull and arrival of charge. At the forty-yard range and at the same twenty-miles-an-hour speed, he will have moved 3.5 feet before the charge arrives. Thus, with your two variable unknowns of his speed and his distance from the gun, you can select a lead amounting to from 2.1 feet to 6.1 feet—nearly a ratio of three to one.

Now, I have a theory about leading which may evoke bellows of protestation from a considerable portion of the gunning fraternity, namely, that more people are inclined to underlead than to overlead.

In the first place, a charge of shot does not, as many people suppose, travel along in the shape of a sphere or even an ellipse. It proceeds in the form of a string several feet long.* Thus, overleading may not be as disastrous as underleading, for some of the shot at the tail of the string may cause the damage which you are trying to effect.

I shall burden you with one more mathematical calculation. Assume a frightened black duck is crossing your line of fire at right angles at 50 miles per hour and at a range of sixty yards. He would be covering about 70 feet per second. You have an express load of 4 shot which will take .2 seconds to reach the line of flight of Mr. Black Duck. The correct lead on this shot, therefore, is 14 feet and longer than that if you are not swinging your gun with the duck.

Many years ago, I had a lesson in long leading when I was invited to participate in a duck shoot at the Clove Valley Club in New York State.

* According to the Western Cartridge Company, 11 to 17 feet long at 60 yards, depending on the load.

There was a hill there, about two or three hundred feet high, at the bottom of which was a good-sized pond, where the ducks lived and were fed. Stand-up blinds consisting of board fences were placed at the base of the hill between the pond and the hill.

The night before the shoot, a number of ducks were trapped and taken to the top of the hill in cages. In the morning, when the gunners were in position, the ducks were released, one cageful at a time, and they flew down the hill over the trees—hell-bent for leather—to get to the water and to breakfast. I might add that the older and wiser walked down and seemed to realize that they were safe when on the ground.

The flying ducks must have been doing far better than fifty miles an hour and, although the range was only about thirty yards, I missed the first five ducks cleanly, even when employing a four-foot lead. My host then suggested that I double my lead. I led the next duck about eight or nine feet and it dropped dead.

These ducks were probably flying at more than 80 feet per second and we were using standard loads with perhaps a 900-foot-per-second integrated velocity. It took this charge about .1 seconds to travel the thirty yards; and, in that length of time the duck moved about eight feet. Q.E.D.

You can learn to lead properly only by experience and educated guess work. The duck won't wait for you to figure it all out on paper. Judgment comes with practice, but one of the attractive things about duck hunting is that this judgment never becomes infallible. One day you'll knock 'em out of the air at fifty yards and the next you'll miss 'em cold at twenty.

If you keep the above figures generally in mind and lean, particularly on the longer shots, toward overleading, I think you will improve your score.

I mentioned wind awhile back. I do not want to burden these pages with too much mathematics, but bear in mind that a steady twenty-mile cross wind can and will move your charge between two and three feet downwind of the point at which you have aimed when shooting at a range of say forty yards. I have never made any measured tests on this, but I have seen a "pot shooter" blast at a duck sitting on the water when a strong cross wind was blowing and have seen the entire charge strike the water downwind of the duck. If the wind is at all strong, remember to allow a little for it. Remember, also, that the fragmented shotgun charge does not have the stabilizing, gyroscopic characteristics of the rapidly rotating rifle bullet and that, even with the latter, allowances have to be made for wind.

In discussing lead so far, we have been considering it in the light of the ideal and theoretical circumstance, in which the duck is traveling at right angles to the line of fire. This often occurs, of course, but the quartering shot—in which the duck is either approaching you or getting farther away as he crosses your field of vision—is, perhaps, the more frequent shot.

Shots of this kind—quartering shots—in which the duck may be gaining or losing altitude, at the same time render it almost obligatory to use the technique of swinging along the line of his flight, passing the duck and gaining and maintaining the lead.

On a quartering shot, of course, the leads should be less than those given in the examples above. A flight angle of forty-five degrees from the line of fire would cut these leads in two; and, if the duck's course is even more *going awayer* or *coming inner* than that, the lead should be less than half.

On the straight going away shot, when the duck is not rising in his line of flight (i.e., is flying horizontally), you should aim ahead of, i.e., under the duck. Of course, if he is a river or pond duck, engaged at the moment, in his skyrocket, vertical rise from the water, you would aim slightly over him. If he is in a gradual climb, so that he stays in your line of sight as you aim at him, you will shoot right at him. We don't want to get into trigonometry—because I have forgotten it too—but I should say that the lead on the straight going away shot is naturally a small lead compared to that used on the cross shot. At a range of twenty-five or thirty yards, and an altitude of, say, thirty feet, on a going away shot if the duck is in horizontal flight, I aim about a foot to eighteen inches *below* the duck. Don't bring your gun down on the duck, because you'll block your view of him. Come up under him and when you are just under him, pull the trigger. Of course, the higher the duck the longer the lead on this shot; and conversely the lower the duck the shorter the lead, until, if he is going straight away from you, just off the water, you naturally aim right at him.

I have referred before to the coming in shot. It is a somewhat difficult shot, because you cannot see the duck when you pull the trigger. Bring your gun up on his line of flight and pass him—i.e., blot him out with your muzzle. Then pull the trigger. It is a temptation to wait too long for this shot. Don't do it. If you are well-concealed and the duck is apparently going right over the top of the blind, shoot before he gets to a distance of about twenty yards. If you wait longer than that your pattern will cover a very small area and you may miss him entirely, or if you do hit him—and it will either be a square hit or none at all—you will pick up nothing but duck hamburger.

Now for a few details:

With a double-barrel gun particularly, put your finger into the guard far enough so that the trigger fits into the crease at the first joint of the finger. If you don't get into the habit of doing this and you pull the trigger with the fatty tip of the finger, someday, when your hand is very cold and numb, the recoil may knock your finger off the front trigger, and as the gun bounces forward again from your shoulder after its recoil, your finger may slip off the front trigger, strike the rear trigger and set off the second barrel.

This is not serious in itself, but it is sloppy shooting, you'll get quite a root in the shoulder and, perhaps worst of all, it will leave you with an empty gun.

Some people have trouble with the trigger guard of the double gun. I had it when I first shifted from the single-trigger, short-trigger guard pump to a double gun. Sometimes I still have it.

The difficulty arises from gripping the small of the stock so tightly that the middle finger of the right hand gets bruised by the rear end of the trigger guard on the side toward the trigger finger. After six or seven shots it becomes really tender and a nice baby mouse will develop. My old ten-bore even cut my finger open a couple of times.

The palliative, but not the cure, is a good thick Band Aid or similar dressing over the mouse. There are two cures:

1. Hold the middle finger at the bottom of the trigger guard, instead of behind it. Personally I find this awkward, and I do not feel at ease with the gun when I do it. It does not bother some people, however, and I think it is worth trying. If it makes you uncomfortable, don't continue it. You must be at ease with your gun.
2. The better cure, I believe, is to hold the gun less tensely with the right hand at the small of the stock. Let the rearward pressure on the gun, to hold it snugly against your shoulder, come from the left hand up on the forearm. The right hand can thus give with the recoil instead of opposing it, and I have found that the uncomfortable mouse will disappear.

People with brachycephalic skulls—that's no disgrace, it just means a wide skull—or with prominent cheekbones, sometimes develop, from the recoil of the gun, a bruise upon the right cheek, usually just below the cheekbone.

There are various cures for this unhappy circumstance, which, if it is allowed to go on too long, will develop into a flinch and spoil your shooting.

One cure, as previously mentioned, is to put more drop in the stock. Another one is to have a good gunsmith or skilled woodworker carve a hollow in the left side of the stock to hold the cheek and the lower, posterior portion of the cheekbone. In some cases, it may be found advisable to cut away some of the comb of the stock.

Lastly—and it is probably not necessary to mention this —hold the gun firmly against the shoulder so that the recoil will not get a head start at you. This does not mean you should pull it back so hard that you create tension or fatigue. Either condition will spoil your swing and thus your shooting.

For every action there is an equal and opposite reaction. The powder burning in the gun pushes the shot forward and the gun backward. The lighter the gun, the less inertia it has for the rearward thrust of the powder to overcome and, thus, the more perceptible the recoil.

The worst kicking gun I ever shot was a little short-barreled, extremely straight 16-gauge owned by a very petite lady, who could not be persuaded that a 12-gauge gun with more weight to it would push her around a lot less.

FIGURE 43 *Second finger placed below trigger guard to avoid being bruised by rear of trigger guard during recoil. If you are comfortable with this position, adopt it. If you are ill at ease with the gun, don't hold it this way. See text.*

For those who desire further knowledge of shotguns and who are interested in making a study of shotgun ballistics as well as the finer points of the handling of shotguns, I can recommend highly George Baekeland's book, *Gunner's Guide*, published by The Macmillan Company, 1948.

One final word about the handling of your gun.

Most of us duck hunters take our guns out of moth balls the day before the season opens. The majority of us probably haven't shot the gun since last year. We lovingly oil up the gun, start out the next morning to shoot a duck and then are surprised and chagrined when we miss the first two or three easy shots.

We should not be surprised, but the emotion of chagrin is entirely in order because it's our own fault.

If, in the course of a year, you drove your car only a few times each fall, and then just backed it out of the driveway and ran it around the block once, you would probably be far from expert at negotiating city traffic or express highways. If you shoot a few dozen shells from your gun on a couple of week ends each fall, you cannot expect to become proficient at that either.

After all, as in all sports, expertness in handling the shotgun results from the development of motor reflexes. You should endeavor to learn to shoot your gun so that when the ducks come in, you need not have half a dozen do's and don't's in mind. If you have, you will be stiff and self-conscious in handling your gun and you will be distracted from the main issues of a clean swing, an accurate determination of lead and hitting the duck. So, if possible, do some trapshooting before the season opens. Train your motor reflexes then and not over the decoys.

Even if it is a warm pre-season day, wear the kind of jacket you would wear were you actually in a blind. A good strong hand trap—the kind with a spring and cocking mechanism, rather than the whip type—is really better for this kind of practice than a standard 16-yard platform trap-shooting setup. The operator of the hand trap can stand around the corner of a building and throw crossing and wide angle birds for you at various angles. From a platform with fixed trap you will get nothing but going away shots. A skeet shoot can be helpful, but the range is really too short and your full-choke duck gun is not suitable for that kind of work.

Do your practicing before the season and not on the ducks themselves. It will pay off in fewer misses and more ducks.

chapter seven

THE CLOTHES

In dressing for the late fall gunning in our unkind New England climate, one must achieve that fine compromise between being moderately comfortable and being not too bulky. I say *moderately* comfortable, because there is no such thing as absolute comfort in gunning north of the thirty-fifth parallel, although one friend of mine approached it several years ago.

He owned a model-A Ford sedan, which was reaching the condition of the One-Horse Shay on its hundredth birthday. He took it down to the shore of a small black-duck pond on his place, removed the salable parts, the steering wheel and column and the glass in the windshield and left it there among the alders. It made a most snug and comfortable blind, inasmuch as the windows still worked. He could—almost—go gunning in boots and pajamas.

In the absence of such a sybaritic blind, we shall have to think about clothes.

The experiments being run by the United States Army and Air Force in Alaska will probably revolutionize our cold-weather dressing habits in the next five or ten years. New materials and the inward reflection of body heat are being studied, and the results will doubtless be of great interest and use to the gunner. Until these new garments become generally available, however, we shall have to garb ourselves more or less in the old-fashioned way.

Let's start at the inside:

If you don't perspire too readily—as I do not—the 100 per cent woolen underwear is, I believe, the best. If, however, you are apt to get damp after a bit of rowing or boat hauling, it might be worth while looking into the double layer underwear made of cotton on the inside and wool on the outside. The cotton absorbs the perspiration and does not seem to be as clammy as wool when it is damp.

I prefer the two-piece underwear—shirt and long drawers—to the so-called union suit. The first reason probably is that I hate to look at myself in a union suit so early in the morning. It is a shock and most destructive of one's self-esteem. The other reason is that the two-piece rig fits snugly around the waist and, to my mind, is not so apt to creep up or down into uncomfortable lumps and creases.

The basic secret, to date, on warm dressing, is to don a multitude of layers. Air is a good insulator and each layer, even of light material, gives you an additional stratum of air. After all, what we are trying to accomplish is to keep the body heat in, rather than to keep the cold out. Thus, two light flannel shirts over the underwear will give you better protection than one heavy one. If it is very cold, wear three; but be sure that they don't bind you in the armpits or over the shoulders. Sweaters are all right, if they are not too snug.

The heavy blanket pants are next. If you can, get them made of unscoured wool, which still contains most of the natural animal oils. These repel water to some extent and are a great comfort when occupying the frost-covered seat of a boat. If the water stands up as little droplets on the cloth, instead of soaking in, you will know that you have the right kind.

I don't like suspenders, or what the British call braces. Unless they stretch very easily, they are apt to restrict the free-

FIGURE 44 *The snugger fitting warm-weather boot.*

FIGURE 45 *The loose fitting cold-weather boot, inside which sheepskin shoes can be worn.*

dom of the movement of your shoulders in swinging a gun. If they do stretch very easily, then you feel as if your pants were coming down each time you have to reach in your pocket for something. A good belt is better.

THE FEET

In gunning the keenest discomfort from the cold occurs in the feet. The basic answer to the problem lies in the loose boot—again the matter of a layer of air.

I keep two pairs of different kinds of boots—one pair for warmer weather about 40 degrees or over, and the other pair for use in temperatures below that. The warm-weather boots are the conventional, rather snug-fitting, black rubber boots—sometimes made in a greyish green. Under these I wear two pairs of socks, the outer pair of which comes up the calf as far as possible, so that the sock will not work down and lump in the bottom of the boot, as it can do if you have to walk very far.

The cold-weather boot is a very large, loose boot with a very short vamp, so that you can get a fur shoe or slipper inside of it. I first put on one pair of wool socks and then a pair of high, loose sheepskin slippers which lace up. These boots, I readily admit, are not too handy for walking long distances and with them you feel a little as if you had diver's boots on. Actually, they are lighter in weight than the warm-weather boots. Their real drawback is that they are bulky and clumsy. If they are big enough to keep you warm, they will drop off your feet an inch or so each time you lift your foot to take a step. Once I had to walk four miles in them on a sand beach. I think I would rather try to climb Mt. Everest than do that again.

In both kinds of boots I put inner soles of sheepskin—fur side up. They help a great deal. I have had boots so large that I could place a thick felt innersole below the sheepskin one. If your feet perspire at all, take out these inner soles when you come in from shooting, put them in a dry place and hang your boots upside down, also in a dry place. Your feet will be warmer when you use the rig the next day because there will be no dampness lurking inside.

There is a third kind of boot—for use only in duck crawling, and pothole hunting—which should have some mention. It is only sixteen or seventeen inches high, made of rubber, very light and flexible and will permit a modest amount of wading. It is good where you have to do a great deal of walking. I am not speaking of the so-called half boot, which is really just the warm-weather boot referred to above, with the top half left out. This is a snug boot with laces over a solid tongue for five inches or so at the top. It is also often laced over a solid tongue at the instep.

Don't ever wear waders.

If you go out in a boat and capsize or fall overboard, the chances are—if you have waders on—that the next nourishment you will take will be embalming fluid.

The Good Lord knows that gunning boots are bad enough in such a predicament; but waders are far worse. They are liable to hold some air as you go into the water and when you come up, it will probably be feet first.

On a muddy or sharply shelving shore, they could give you a nasty time if you fell down and got them filled with water.

You've doubtless read of trout fishermen on swift streams who have been drowned by them.

Don't wear 'em.

THE HANDS

Next to the feet, the hands can probably cause more agony from the cold, than any other part of the body. The heart has to pump blood through long pipe lines to them.

First, I believe in wristlets. The blood is near the surface at the wrist, and it loses a lot of heat if your wrists are exposed to the cold. Next time your wife or your girl wants to knit you a pair of socks, ask her to make wristlets. Three to four inches long is about right; and if there is an old piece of any kind of fur kicking around the sewing basket, ask that they be lined with that, with the fur side in. They will make all the difference in the world to your comfort, particularly to your right hand, from which, if there are many ducks about, you will be stripping your glove or mitten every few minutes.

Incidentally, if it is very cold, I usually rub my hands with lamb or beef fat before I set out. It seems to me that they don't get so cold when I do. Don't use bacon or ham fat. They have a lot of salt in them, and that does not seem to help any.

I don't like mittens. I'll admit that they are warmer; but they are so clumsy when it comes to handling anything that I find that I am taking them off all the time, and thus my hands get colder than they do with gloves, which lend some residual dexterity and which don't have to be removed so often. I use a heavy leather glove with a wool lining and, in the coldest weather, the sheepskin glove with the wool turned in.

I have tried gloves and mittens made with a slit in the right palm so, presumably, you can stick out your trigger finger and shoot with your glove on. They don't work—for me—anyway. Your grip on the gun is unnatural and uncomfortable and thus you become distracted from the main issue, which is to hit the duck.

FIGURE 46 *The pocket warmer closed—bag removed.*

FIGURE 47 *Pocket warmer open, showing wick burner.*

By all means take two or three pairs of gloves with you. I keep a pair of large, long rubber gloves in my gunning bag, with a pair of wool ones inside. These I wear when setting out or picking up decoys. While you are doing this, don't leave your other gloves in the blind. Stuff them inside your coat or shirt where they will keep warm.

One of the handiest gadgets, which has come upon the market recently, is the hand or pocket warmer. It is a boon to the gunner.

It consists of a flat metal can about the size of a cigarette case, which pulls apart into two sections. One section, which is perforated to permit the entrance of oxygen, is just a cover. The other contains cotton which is saturated with lighter fluid, just like a cigarette lighter. On top of this section is a small asbestos burner which, I imagine, contains a hair or two of fine platinum wire. Platinum will oxidize so rapidly in the vapors of gasoline that it will become incandescent. You fill the warmer with lighter fluid, shake out the excess, replace the burner and start the process going with the flame of a match or cigarette lighter, held at the side of the burner—not under it, because a carbon

FIGURE 48 *The alpaca jacket. Sleeves are lined with the same material.*

deposit seems to render it inoperative. You put the top on and put the whole device into a little flannelette bag, which comes with the gadget.

The best way, to my mind, to use the warmer is to have another bag made of some soft, warm windproof cloth—again a double layer will turn the trick. This bag should be big enough so that you can insert your hand and the warmer easily, but not so big as to be draughty. Sling this bag from your belt so that it hangs down inside the top of your right boot, in front.

With this rig, you can leave off your right glove—but stuff it inside your clothes—and can keep your right hand warm and snug in the bag until it is time to shoot.

Of course, if you have slit breast pockets in the front of your jacket, you can keep it in there and pull the same stunt.

THE JACKET

You will note that I use the term "jacket" instead of the word "coat."

I don't like a long coat for gunning. Every time you get up and sit down again, you will find yourself squirming around, as if you had ants in your pants, trying to get the long coat smooth and comfortable under your tail. Furthermore, unless

FIGURE 49 *The correct length for the alpaca gunning jacket.*

you pull it out to the rear, as you sit down, it will stand away from the back of your neck and the cold north wind will play arpeggios up and down your spine. In a boat it is an impossible garment.

So get yourself a jacket which is as long as it can be without getting under your tail when you sit down. Some jackets are made with a let-down flap at the back to sit on. This is a convenience on wet or frosty mornings, but I have never seen this attachment on what I consider the ideal jacket, described in the next paragraph.

The alpaca pile jacket with a waterproof or water-repellent outer layer is, in my opinion, the most satisfactory. It is light and flexible and gives you the freedom of action which you must have to handle your gun properly. Get it big enough. Get it too big. Then it won't bind you anywhere. Be sure that the sleeves are lined with alpaca and not with some nonprotecting cloth. This is important to the comfort of your arms and hands.

A few manufacturers make pants lined with alpaca pile. These are extremely warm and seem to be more comfortable and flexible than the standard heavy woolen pants mentioned above. Their only drawback is their cost. The ones which I have seen are quite expensive.

If possible, get the jacket with a hood, not that you can possibly shoot properly in a hood, but in the lulls, when the ducks are flying somewhere else, you will find it a great comfort.

Be sure that you don't buy a jacket that is too light in color, so that every movement you make will be the more easily discernible by the ducks. Get a good neutral grayish or greenish brown, which will blend into the blind and into the background.

Keep away from the leather jackets and the sheepskin-lined ones. They are all too stiff and clumsy and will make you miss a lot of birds. They are usually particularly binding around the shoulders and armpits—just where you most need the greatest freedom.

If your jacket fits you correctly for gunning, it should be loose, and you should feel like a young cat who can turn halfway around inside his own skin.

THE CAP

You are not deer hunting or shooting pheasants, so don't wear a bright red cap or a cap of any bright contrasting color.

The gray-green corduroy cap, with let-down ear flaps, which was so popular a few decades ago, is very good, except that it does get sodden in the rain. I wear a dull green leather cap, which sheds water and blends with the background.

Of course, the main disadvantage of a cap is that half the water which it sheds goes down the back of your neck. Wearing an old felt hat will obviate this, but it should be of a neutral shade and you will not find it very cosy if the temperature is below freezing. Your ears will get brittle if there is much wind; also your hood cannot be slipped over it.

RAIN CLOTHES

Don't wear bright yellow oilers.

I am not sure whether or not the spectral sensitivity of the retina of a duck is more or less the same as that of homo sapiens, to whom yellow is one of the most distinctive and, let us say irritating, colors.

At the end of World War II, there were, on the market, a lot of light canvas rain suits, which had been made for the Navy and for the Coast Guard. I have a couple of them and do not think that they are very much good, in spite of the fact that their color is neutral. In a light rain they will serve; but in a downpour they become saturated after about an hour.

The old-fashioned short black rubber coat and pants are about the best compromise for rain clothes; but try to get the pants with a drawstring instead of the overall-like bib and suspenders so they won't bind your shoulders. The more expensive plastic rain suits—two piece, of course—are even better because they are lighter and more flexible and give you greater freedom of action. However, be sure that they are dark or neutral in color.

Don't try to gun in a long raincoat. It has all the disadvantages applying to the long coat, which were discussed under the Section on Jackets. If you use the two-piece variety, you will be much happier and will enjoy greater freedom of movement.

CARTRIDGE BELTS

These are not strictly clothes, but you wear 'em, so I guess that they should be referred to at this point.

Some jackets come with cartridge loops on them, but they are usually placed too high up to be really handy. Furthermore, the loops are generally made of cloth or canvas, which gets tacky and shrinks tight around the shells when it rains. A man trying to get shells out of one of these coats on a rainy day looks to me like a monkey in a zoo with a bad attack of fleas.

I don't believe in carrying shells in the pockets.

In the first place, they cannot be removed as quickly as they can from a cartridge belt and, in the second place, they can get marred and dented, which condition—if you use a pump or an automatic—can cause a jam.

I like the cartridge belt. Its location is handy. It protects the shells. You can put different shot sizes in different parts of the belt and know, simply by their location what size shot you are putting in your gun.

The leather ones are preferable to the web ones because the rain does not affect them. Give the leather belt a drink of saddle soap once a year, and it will last probably as long as you will.

FIGURE 50 *The leather cartridge belt.*

chapter eight

DESCRIPTIONS OF THE MORE USUAL DUCKS AND SOME OF THEIR HABITS

This is not an ornithological book, and I want to make it perfectly clear that I am not an ornithologist. If I did not do so, it would be apparent to you, anyway, before you finished this chapter.

It is my aim here to deal only in the most superficial way with the ducks you may encounter from day to day; but I have attempted to include the most important distinguishing characteristics between species and subspecies. If I succeed, thereby, in arousing your interest, so that you make a further study of the subject, this chapter will have served its purpose.

If you want to make such further study, I believe that the finest book on the subject is: *The Ducks, Geese and Swans of North America*, by Francis H. Kortright, published by American Wildlife Institute, Washington, D. C. 1942, 1943.

The minute descriptions and the excellent color plates in this volume will answer almost any question which can arise in your mind.

For quite good color plates and brief descriptions, Roger Tory Peterson's book, *A Field Guide to the Birds*, Houghton, Mifflin Company, is a convenient and very helpful book.

When I shoot a duck, I am never satisfied until I determine to what species he belongs and what his Christian name and surname are.

All ducks fall into five subfamilies of the great family *Anatidae*, which includes the swans and the geese and brant. We shall deal here—and briefly—only with these five subfamilies.

I. River or Pond Ducks
(ANATINAE)

The most frequently encountered of these are:

The black duck
The mallard
The baldpate (generally called widgeon)
The pintail
The blue-winged teal and the green-winged teal
The cinnamon teal
The shoveller
The gadwall
The wood duck

These are the dabbling ducks which feed generally on vegetable matter and thus make better eating. They feed usually in shallow water by standing on their heads, with their tails in the air. They seldom dive except when they are in danger or wounded, in which cases they can swim excellently under water.

There are two infallible ways in which to distinguish these ducks from those of the other subfamilies:

1. In taking off from the water, particularly when alarmed, they spring up vertically for several feet before assuming horizontal flight.
2. The feet of these ducks differ from the feet of all others.

All ducks have four toes—three forward, which are webbed, and one small toe aft. The hind toe on these ducks has no web or lobe to it.

All of these ducks are perfectly delicious if they have not been eating duck clams.

II. Bay, Sea or Diving Ducks
(NYROCINAE)

The more usual of these are:

The canvasback
The redhead
The bufflehead (sometimes called the butterball)
The greater scaup and the lesser scaup (generally referred to as the big bluebill and the little bluebill).
The American goldeneye (generally referred to as the whistler).
The eiders
The old squaw
The harlequin
The three scoters, white-winged, American and surf (referred to generally and erroneously as coot*).

The canvasback is the most delicious of all ducks and I doubt that anyone will dispute that statement.

The Scoter tribe are, in my opinion, practically inedible, except in stew form; and, so far as I am concerned, you have to have a tough gizzard to eat 'em even then.

These bay, sea and diving ducks dive for their food and also have two other marked characteristics for identification.

1. When they take off from the water they patter along the surface for a ways—like a seaplane—instead of rising vertically as do the river and pond

* The true coot has a yellow, or blue or gray bill shaped like a crow's. He is small—as small as a teal. His feet are not webbed but have instead little folding paddles, one to each tarsal of each of his three front toes. His legs are set very far aft. He is usually a solid black, but I have seen a few gray ones. He is sometimes referred to as the mud hen. He does not fly much and usually swims in compact flocks of as many as five hundred. By reputation, he is inedible; but friends of mine, who have tried him, say that he is delicious. Being a vegetarian, he should be.

clan. The Scoters almost always fly close to the water.

2. The hind toe has a clear and distinct web or lobe on its under side.*

III. Mergansers
(MERGINAE)

We find three kinds of mergansers in North America: the hooded, the American and the red-breasted.

In hand, identification of this duck cannot be missed. He has a long narrow bill with built-in saw teeth slanting to the rear, the better to hold his finny diet when he catches it.

In the air he is a long rangy bird, but the great amount of white on him may, at certain angles, make you confuse him with the goldeneye or greater scaup.

He is edible, if you'll do certain things to him, as set forth in the chapter on cleaning, cooking and eating.

IV. Ruddy Ducks
(ERISMATURINAE)

These are very small ducks, about the size of the teal, only chunkier. Although they possess the lobed hind toe of the bay, sea or diving ducks, they are essentially fresh-water ducks. The legs are set so far aft that they can hardly walk on land.

In hand, the ruddy duck can be readily identified by his tail which consists of very stiff coarse feathers. He often has a longer tail for his size than other ducks. In swimming, this tail is sometimes erected almost vertically, like a small fan. The chin and cheeks of both the male and the female are white.

V. Tree Ducks
(DENDROCYGNINAE)

This long-legged duck appears only in the extreme southerly part of Central and Far Western United States. There are two varieties: the fulvous and the black-bellied.

* This feature is shared also by mergansers and ruddy ducks.

Those who are so inclined can skip the next few pages, because they are intended principally for reference to aid you in identifying ducks which you have shot and to inform you of a few of their habits. For the sake of brevity, I shall not repeat the broad identifying features mentioned above.

This is only a rough guide to the various duck species one is likely to encounter, and it should be fortified with a good book on the subject.

All ducks molt twice a year. The first molt is in late spring or early summer, after the breeding season, when the male doffs his usually brighter colors and assumes the more modest dress of the female. This is known as the "eclipse" plumage and in acquiring it both sexes lose their flight feathers and cannot fly for some time.

In early fall the winter plumage comes out again and is retained until late the next spring.

The following very brief descriptions deal only with the winter plumage. After all, that is usually the only costume in which the average gunner ever sees a duck.

THE BLACK DUCK

The black duck is not black. He merely appears to be so, from a distance, except for the touches of silver under his wings, which can be observed only when he is in the air. Actually, instead of being black, he is of a dusky, brownish, bronzelike color. The head and neck have a lighter tone with a creamy cast. The wing has a bluish-purplish iridescent speculum, i.e., a patch on the side of the wing.

The drake and the hen are the same in appearance, but some people claim that the drake has one or two upward and forward curling feathers on his back at the base of his tail. I have seen them on some ducks.

The hen has a hearty quack, which I think I can distinguish from the quack of the hen mallard, because, in general, its cadence seems a little slower than that of the mallard. The drake can utter only a low, hoarse, "greep, greep."

They are large birds, 21 to 25 inches measured from bill to tip of tail along the back.

Eminent ornithologists differ as to whether the so-called red-leg or Canadian black duck, which one does not see until late in the fall, is a different and separate subspecies, or whether it is merely an older common black duck with its winter plumage further developed. I don't know the answer, although I have shot both kinds of ducks in the same day, and shall describe only the main differences between them:

> The common black duck is smaller with olive-greenish feet and bill.
>
> The red-leg black duck is a considerably larger bird with yellowish bill and bright light red feet.

THE MALLARD

The mallard domesticates easily. You have probably seen so many of them in city parks that they need little description here.

The mallard ranges in size from the common black duck to the red-leg black duck, and the shape of the two species is very much the same. The hen mallard, however, is a light stippled brown. The drake, in winter plumage, has a dark green iridescent head, usually a thin necklace of pure white and a dark throat and breast. The body is gray and the belly appears white in flight. The speculum has white bars.

Their respective voices are about the same as the voices of the black ducks.

Mallards and blacks frequently interbreed—my half wild ones do—and their offspring will have all kinds of gradations of color between the limits of the two parents.

THE CINNAMON TEAL

This is a very small duck found only on the Pacific Coast. The male, as the name would indicate, is a cinnamon color. The female is a small brown duck similar in over-all coloration to the female mallard, but much smaller.

Both male and female have blue wing patches. They are about the same size as the blue-winged teal.

THE SHOVELER

This duck—often called the spoonbill—needs but scant description. It is slightly smaller than the common black duck.

Marked somewhat like the mallard in both sexes, except for the reddish belly of the male, its main and unmistakable feature is its long spatulate bill.

It is but rarely found in the Northeast.

THE GADWALL

This duck seldom comes into New England and usually, on the East Coast, stays south of Chesapeake Bay.

The male is a grayish duck with a brown head and neck. The best distinguishing feature, in hand, is the dark patch bordered with white on the rear edge of the wing. Forward of this patch is another of chestnut-colored feathers.

The female in general coloration and conformation is much like the female pintail and the female mallard. The chestnut patch on the wing of the female gadwall, while smaller than that on the male, will distinguish this duck from the two other species.

The gadwall is smaller than the common black duck and runs from 19 to 21 inches in length.

THE BALDPATE

This bird, in our part of the country, is called the widgeon.

He is considerably smaller than the mallard or the black, 18 to 22 inches.

The white top of the head of the male gives this duck its name. The male also has a white patch on his side just forward of the tail. Both male and female are a grayish brown and the head of the female has a creamy tinge to it, which is not obvious at any distance.

In hand, one of the strongest distinguishing features is the short bill.

In flight, they flash a great deal of white from breast, belly and the light gray underwing. They are very nervous and erratic in the air, changing both altitude and direction constantly.

THE AMERICAN PINTAIL

This duck—now rare in New England and much more plentiful on the West Coast—is of good size, 24 to 30 inches. Perhaps the most outstanding feature, outside of that which gives him his name, is his comparatively long neck.

The male has a gray body and a dark brown head, a white neck and a long spike tail. The female is a stippled brown, like the female mallard, but has a much more pointed tail. Neither has the white barred specula on the wings, which are exhibited by the mallard. The pintail's neck is much longer.

In flight, the wings are long and sharp pointed. There is also a white edging at the rear of the wing.

THE TEAL

Of the two teal seen in these parts—the green-winged and the blue-winged—the latter is slightly larger, 15 to 17 inches.

The green-winged teal is named for the bright green iridescent specula on the wings of both males and females. The male has a similar green patch about the eye and on the back of his neck. His sides are grayish; the breast and belly are whitish and his head has a reddish tone and a small crest. The bill is black.

The female has a brownish buff body and a dark mark running fore and aft through the eye. Her belly is whitish. Her bill is slightly lighter in tone than that of the male.

The blue-winged teal, the larger bird, is similar in general appearance and also has an iridescent green speculum in both sexes; but above the speculum, and running to the forward edge of the wing are feathers of a beautiful cobalt blue.

In hand, you cannot miss the correct identification of these little ducks.

THE WOOD DUCK

The male wood duck is the most beautiful of all the ducks. The head is greenish, striped with white, blending into an iridescent blue at sides and rear. The back is greenish blue and the breast, reddish.

The female is a brownish gray duck with light breast. The two best distinguishing marks, in hand, are the dark yellow feet and the legs and the deep yellow eyelids of both the male and the female.

These are medium-sized ducks—16 to 20 inches. They are found in swamps and rivers and make their nests in hollow trees.

THE CANVASBACK

This duck—the most comestible of all ducks—is becoming rare in these parts.

They are good-sized ducks—20 to 25 inches.

They have large heads distinguished by the almost straight line slope from crown to end of bill. On most ducks this line is an inward curve.

In the male the head and neck are reddish. The sides and back are a stippled gray, light in tone.

The head and neck of the female are somewhat lighter in their reddish tones.

In flight the male appears bigger and whiter than the female.

THE REDHEAD

The redhead is also becoming rare hereabouts.

As one might suspect from the name, this duck has a red head and you might, if you were careless, confuse it, even in the hand, with the canvasback. However, the high, almost puffy effect of the crown of the head and the sharp inward curve of the line of the forehead and bill, render such an error unlikely if the powers of observation are exercised to any degree.

The male redhead is a darker and smaller duck than the canvasback. So is the female; but her head is lighter than that of the male redhead and her body is more brown than gray.

THE BUFFLEHEAD

Frequently called the butterball, this small duck is a chunky little fellow, with an oversized head and a small bill protruding almost at right angles from the forehead. His length runs from 12 to 15 inches.

The male has a white breast and belly, a large white spot running to the top of his head from behind the eye. He is supposed to have splashes of green, red and purple on his head; but although I have shot many of them, I have never seen this neon-light effect. Perhaps the bufflehead have moved to the south'ard of me, before they reach this stage of their winter plumage. He has a large white patch—more than a speculum—on the top of the wing.

The female is slightly smaller than the male and her feathers are a grayish brown. Her breast and belly are a light gray. She, too, has a white spot on her head; but it runs from behind the eye, slightly downward.

THE GREATER SCAUP AND THE LESSER SCAUP

More usually called the big and little bluebill, the greater runs in length 17 to 20 inches, the lesser 15 to 18 inches.

The head, neck and chest of the male of both subspecies are almost black and the head is slightly iridescent. The bill is a dull, gray, turquoise blue. The back is a stippled gray and the belly is white. Each has a white band on the top of the wing nearer the trailing edge; but the band of the greater scaup is longer and runs farther toward the tip of the wing.

The females of both subspecies are brown ducks. The bills are blue like those of the males, the bellies white. The handiest distinguishing mark on the female of both subspecies is the white ring on the face around the base of the bill. The best way to distinguish between the females of the two subspecies is by the longer line of white feathers on the wing of the greater scaup.

THE AMERICAN GOLDENEYE

This duck is often called the whistler, because in a chill, still December dawn you can hear the pulsating whistle of his wings a mile away. His flight is very rapid, so rapid that if the pitch of his whistle is rising, you will know—even before you can see him—that he is coming toward you, and, if it is dropping, you can be sure that he is going away. It is a magic and wonderful sound.

The male has a bright blackish-green head, high crowned and puffy at the top. There is a white spot in front of and somewhat below his eye. The back is dark grayish-black; but his underparts are white and in flight he is one of the whitest ducks that you will see.

The female has a reddish-brown head, which might lead you to confuse her with the female redhead. The white, or near white collar of the goldeneye will distinguish them for you. The collar does not meet at the back. Also the eye, as the name indicates, is a bright gold color in both sexes. The eye of the redhead is brown.

The body of the female goldeneye is grayish brown and the belly light gray.

THE EIDERS

There are six subspecies of eiders.

Steller's eider, the spectacled eider, the Pacific eider and the northern eider spend the entire year in the far north and only the American and king eiders come as far south as the New England coast. These are rugged sea ducks and seldom come into ponds or inland waters.

The principal distinguishing mark of both the American and king eider is the growth of the horny structure of the bill in rounded plates up each side of the forward portion of the face.

This horny structure is quite wide and broadly rounded at the top in the case of the male king eider.

The male of the American eider has a white back and dark under parts and the back of the head has light green markings. The female is brown. Both have head structures in which the bill and forehead form more or less a straight line. The American eider runs in size from 20 to 26 inches and is slightly larger than the king eider.

The male king eider has a reddish bill with a sharp curve between it and the forehead. His cheeks are light green, breast white, and rear parts dull brown. The female is brown and can be distinguished from the female American eider by the pronounced curve between bill and forehead.

THE OLD SQUAW

The old squaw, size 17 to 21 inches, has a white head, the male having a dark splash below and behind the eye. The male has considerable white on the back with patches of brown and a brown breast. The female has a brown back. Bellies of both are white. The tips of the bills of both have slight downward hooks upon them.

THE HARLEQUIN DUCK

The eastern and western harlequin ducks have the same plumage and appearance. They are about the size of the blue-winged teal.

The male is a slate blue with red and white markings on both head and body.

The female is a brown duck with lighter breast and cheeks and two white markings, one ahead of and one behind the eye. She might be confused with the female bufflehead but the latter has only one white spot on her head and that is aft of the eye.

THE SCOTERS

American, White-Winged and Surf

These are big, heavy, chunky sea birds. The biggest is the white-winged, 20 to 23 inches. The surf is slightly smaller and the American slightly smaller still.

All scoters have a distinguishing hump on the top of the bill, in varying degrees.

The males are easy to differentiate. All three are black, but the American has an orange lump at the top of the base of the bill. The white-winged has a white patch on the top of the wing and a white mark surrounding the eye. The surf has a white patch on his forehead.

The female American is a brown bird with lighter brown cheeks and neck. The female white-winged is similar, but has a white patch on the wing. The surf female is lighter in her brown shade, except for the crown of her head, which is dark, and she has a lighter spot at the back of her head.

THE RUDDY DUCK

This duck has already been described on page 116.

THE MERGANSERS

American, Hooded and Red-Breasted

The principal distinguishing marks of the Mergansers have already been set forth on page 116, but it might be well to describe briefly the main differences between the three subspecies.

The biggest is the American, 20 to 27 inches. Slightly smaller is the red-breasted and the hooded is smallest of all, 17 to 19 inches.

The males, again, are the more easily distinguished.

Both the American and the red-breasted have green heads, but the latter has a scraggly crest extending aft from the top and back of his head, and a stippled reddish chest. The American has a pinkish tinge to his chest and belly, but no stippling. The hooded has a black head and a fan-shaped crest with a white mark in the center.

The females of the American and the red-breasted are difficult to tell apart. They both have reddish heads, gray backs and white breasts and bellies. Perhaps the best way to make a guess as to the identification is to judge by the crests. The crest on the American protrudes aft from the back of the head. The crest of the red-breasted is double and, although it also points aft, it springs from the crown.

The female hooded is, of course, smaller and its crest is partially fan shaped like that of the male of this subspecies.

THE SPEECH OF DUCKS

Black Duck

MALE: A low "greep, greep."

FEMALE: Loud strident "quack" slower in cadence than that of mallard.

These and the mallards are the most loquacious of all ducks.

Mallard

Both male and female substantially the same as black ducks, except quack of female slightly faster in cadence.

Baldpate

MALE: Three musical notes "whew, whew, whew."

FEMALE: "Quawk, quawk."

Pintail

MALE: In flight only, a loud, "qua, qua."

FEMALE: A rare, hoarse "quack."

Green-Winged Teal

MALE: A whistle–soft, sometimes twittering.
FEMALE: A low, faint "quack."

Blue-Winged Teal

MALE: In flight only, a frequently repeated whistling "peep."
FEMALE: Similar to female green-winged, but fainter.

Cinnamon Teal

Rarely speaks. Male utters a chatter of very low volume. Female a weak "quack."

Gadwall

MALE: A loud "kack, kack."
FEMALE: A loud "quack," pitched higher than that of the mallard.

Shoveler

Usually silent. Male has a clucking sound, female a low "quack."

Redhead

MALE: Usually silent in the autumn.
FEMALE: A "quack" similar to female mallard, but higher and infrequent.

Wood Duck

A loquacious duck who chuckles, squeaks and whistles. To the best of my knowledge the hen does not "quack."

Canvasback

MALE: A guttural croak or a peeping. Does not speak often.

FEMALE: A "quack" similar to female mallard.

Greater Scaup

MALE AND FEMALE: "Scaup-scaup." Also a trilling "Prrr."

Lesser Scaup

MALE AND FEMALE: Speak usually only at night or at early dawn—a trilling "Prrr" same as greater scaup.

American Goldeneye

MALE AND FEMALE: Usually silent. The whistle of the wings is, of course, unmistakable. The female can "quack" when startled.

Bufflehead

MALE AND FEMALE: Usually silent.

American Eider

MALE: A call slightly reminiscent of an owl only lower and rougher in tone. The female can "quack."

Old Squaw

A very talkative duck with quite a variety in its vocabulary, makes a chattering sound filled with vowels.

Harlequin Duck

A high squeaky voice like a mouse.

White-Winged Scoter

MALE AND FEMALE: Silent when sitting. Sometimes a low whistle in flight.

Surf Scoter

MALE AND FEMALE: Rarely speak. Sometimes utter a low croak.

American Scoter

MALE AND FEMALE: A rare low hooting whistle.

Mergansers

All three, hooded, American and red-breasted are silent birds, uttering only rarely a hoarse croak.

Ruddy Duck

In the autumn, both male and female are silent.

SOME OTHER HABITS

The common black duck, particularly, will spend the night in some cove or mudhole and will usually wing his way out to sea or the center of some large body of water at dawn. During the first few days of the gunning season your decoys may deceive him and he may come in close enough for a shot. But after that, all is different. He is the most intelligent of all the ducks, and he learns quickly and apparently remembers well. After the first few days, you will probably get more blacks at potholes than you will over decoys.

The red-leg black performs quite differently, at times. The recent migrants from Canada often act like boys from the country and are frequently ingenuous about decoys. They have probably been living in a country where there are few men. These are the ducks most often deluded by the shadow decoy described in the chapter on Duck Deception.

The mallard is somewhat similar to the common black duck in his habits; but I have never believed that he has the intellectual capacity of the black.

The teal are the dunces of the pond and river clan. They will flop down into your decoys as readily as the merganser, who also decoys very well, particularly if the flock consists of only two, three or four birds.

The teal are not discriminating ducks and appear to me to be less easily alarmed than most of the good eating ducks—with the exception of the bufflehead, whose nickname woolhead is well earned.

Don't underestimate, however, the ability of a teal to get off the water and out of gunshot in no time flat. Many times I have had a pair of teal settle in the stool, have stood up to put them in the air—which they take to like a pair of skyrockets—and have knocked down the first bird and missed the second cold because, by the time I swung to him, he was so far away that he escaped through the gaps in my pattern. (Of course, I might not have been on him.)

The scaup—greater and lesser—are our most numerous, early season, bay, sea or diving ducks.

They are very temperamental ducks, in that today they will pile up over your stool and tomorrow will flare away from it at a hundred-yard range. Furthermore, they possess—to the greatest degree—one of the most discouraging and disappointing habits of ducks.

All ducks will dive when wounded and particularly if pursued. If the bottom is weedy, they will grab weeds, hang on and drown themselves. It seems to me, however, that both the scaup do this more frequently than any other duck, with the possible exception of the goldeneye. In the next chapter we shall deal with the method of trying to avert such calamities.

The bufflehead, whose I.Q. may be expressed only in minus numbers, will fly or swim into the decoys. If you shoot at him and miss him, he may patter off a hundred yards or so and resume his diving for his lunch.

The least perceptive to danger, however, seems to be the scoter tribe—especially the surf scoter. Sometimes, even when the shot spatters all around him, he won't fly.

The merganser decoys as well as the best of them, and he is a fast and sporting bird to shoot at. He is perceptive to danger, although not in the same class, with regard to his apprehension, as the black duck or even the scaup.

The goldeneye is not a gregarious bird. You will seldom see more than half a dozen at a time; and usually you will observe singles and pairs. The singles and pairs often will decoy quite well. The larger groups are inclined to be snobbish. In my opinion, the goldeneye will fly off with, or swim off with, more lead than will any other duck.

The Canada goose should receive some mention in this work, although it is primarily aimed at the duck.

Here is the most intelligent of all the water fowl. There is always an old gander who is boss man and dictator of the flock or—as they used to say in fifteenth-century England—the gaggle of geese. The powers of perception of danger of these old leaders are almost psychic. Once in a while, if you are extremely well concealed in your water blind, and the old gander is off his feed a bit that day, you may get a shot at a straggling goose. Don't shoot the gander, who will be at the apex of the "V." He will probably prove to be about as edible as a 7 x 20 truck tire.

If there is a field of winter rye in your vicinity, that may prove to be the best location to hunt geese. Corn shooks, a hollowed-out haystack, or a masked hole in the ground (which the owner of the field will doubtless dislike) can serve as a blind.

Use 2 shot or BB's and plenty of patience. Since federal regulations outlawed flyers, goose hunting is not what it was.

Some reference should also be made to the brant. There are two varieties, the American and the black, the former being found usually on the East Coast and the latter on the West Coast. Both are of the goose family.

The brant is a small salt-water goose, not much bigger than a mallard duck, with black head, neck and foreparts. The American has a light belly and the Black a dark belly. They are rarely found on fresh water and seem to prefer wild rugged sea coasts.

In flight they do not form the orderly "V" of the Canada geese, nor have they the distinguishing "honk" of their larger relatives. They are often loquacious in the air, uttering a confused babbling, which sounds somewhat like a pack of dogs barking in the distance.

ON THE WING

The identification of birds on the wing is a difficult art, the inaccuracy of which increases at a rate about equal to the cube of the distance between you and the bird.

The first steps of differentiating between ducks and the other air borne creatures are not too difficult. One readily learns to detect the flexible and comparatively slow wing action of the herring gull and the long energy-conserving soaring glide of the various members of the so-called hawk family, many of whom are really Buteos or buzzards. It is easy to learn to identify the crow, who almost always flies as if he were falling down stairs. Geese, because of their size, formation in flight and leisurely wing strokes, cannot be mistaken for other birds. Beyond this point, however, the problem becomes increasingly difficult.

I have seen people with appreciable gunning experience confuse loons and cormorants with ducks. The loon's neck is long, the wings rather shallow fore and aft, and the neck has a downward curve. The wing action, although faster than that of a cormorant, is slower than that of a duck.

The cormorant appears even darker than a loon, his neck is longer and his wings are deeper. Sitting on the water, he assumes a snobbish air and elevates his bill at an angle of nearly forty-five degrees. His long neck stands high above the waves. The loon floats very low in the water.

The black duck has an indescribable, but distinctive and rather rapid wing action, although it is not so fast as that of the bay, sea and diving ducks or that of the smaller river or pond ducks. If you are close enough to him, you can see the silver linings of his wings.

At a distance the black and the mallard cannot be differentiated. Closer to, the mallard will appear lighter in color.

The baldpate shows much white in flight and his course of flight is ever-changing and erratic.

The pintail can be identified first, of course, by his long spike tail, which is not so marked in the female. His wings, to me, seem to slant further to the rear, like those of a jet plane.

The teal have a very rapid—perhaps the most rapid—wing action and appear to be very small in the air.

If the gadwall is close enough to you, the white patch on the trailing edge of the wings will be apparent.

The line of the canvasback's neck, head and bill will distinguish him for you, if he is close enough. His neck is long; but so is the merganser's. However, the merganser will show perhaps more white and his wings do not appear to be set so far aft. Canvasbacks often fly in a long straight line.

Three of the most readily confused ducks in the mid distance are the scaup, the goldeneye and the merganser. This is probably due mostly to the fact that each of them exhibits considerable white when in flight. If the goldeneye is upwind of you, you can, of course, hear the whistle of his wings. Perhaps the confusion arises because, as Julius Caesar said, "All men believe that which they wish to believe." We see a merganser flashing white at two hundred yards. We wish he were a highly comestible scaup. He comes in to stool. We believe that he is a scaup and continue in such belief until we lift the merganser from the water.

We should not confuse them because the merganser is much longer and rangier than the rather chunky scaup; but we do—at least I do, often.

The three scoters are confusing. At any distance they are indistinguishable, and I have seen experienced people confuse them with blacks and other ducks. The scoter's wing action is slower and his flight is not so rapid as that of the black. As previously mentioned, he usually flies low to the water.

The bufflehead and the ruddy duck can easily be confused. Both are small and fly close to the water. Both are often found in large flocks of fifty or more and swim close together.

Near by, or through glasses, the white markings on the top of the head of the bufflehead will help in identification as will the white mark behind the eye of his mate; but the male ruddy duck has white cheeks and the female ruddy, too, has light-colored cheeks. In flight the bufflehead will show white wing patches. The ruddy duck has none. The fan-shaped, nearly vertical tail of the ruddy, often exhibited when sitting on the water, will assist you in distinguishing between the species.

Both scaup and baldpate, when flying in large snarls in the far or far-middle distance, will appear to twinkle and shimmer in the air. This is probably due to the fact that the white portions of these ducks are alternately exposed and concealed by the wing action.

chapter nine

HALF AN HOUR BEFORE SUNRISE

As Benjamin Franklin said, "A little neglect may breed mischief: for want of a nail the shoe was lost; for want of a shoe the horse was lost; and for want of a horse the rider was lost."

This applies to duck hunting as well as to the less important aspects of life.

Back in days of market gunning, when the ducks "blackened the skies," it did not make so much difference if, by error in judgment, or by carelessness, you missed a duck or two. Fifty more would be along in just a minute.

Now it is different—entirely different. The Fates, who regulate the fortunes of Nimrod Anas, do not hand out as many opportunities per diem as they used to; and, thus, full advantage must be taken of each one.

If you have the irritated feeling that this book has gone into far too much detail, remember that it does so with intention and with due regard for wise old Benjamin Franklin's sage advice.*

If it is cloudy, be *at* your blind an hour before sunrise.

* Which, incidentally, he cribbed from George Herbert, who wrote the lines a century before.

If it is clear and Orion's Belt and the spilling Great Dipper of late fall are shining above you, as you leave the warm fireside, it is wise to be at your blind an hour and twenty or more minutes before sunrise.

The federal regulations prohibit shooting earlier than one half an hour before sunrise, and I am not advocating that you violate the law. However, there are several other reasons why you should get to your blind in plenty of time.

First, it usually takes longer than you think to set your stool properly, especially if you have to use a boat to do it. Second, it stimulates the ducks' instinct of self-preservation if, in the perfectly adequate pre-sunrise light you are flopping about in the water, setting your stool, or marching up and down the shore. Ducks often—although not always—start moving as soon as they can see, and your noisy and movement-filled presence is not going to assure them that your body of water is a good place to settle down on for breakfast.

Thus, by the time you can see any distance, your stool should be set, your boat camouflaged, and you should be concealed in your blind.

Incidentally, don't leave your car near the blind. Hide it in high woods or brush, if you can. If you are gunning in bare country, try to camouflage the car with brush or branches brought along for the purpose. If that is too bothersome, bring along an old neutral-colored tarp or a flock of burlap bags, opened and fastened together, to cover the car. The fine collection of bathroom chromium with which the modern car is graced will, with its glinting response to the sun, warn the ducks that all is not well in your vicinity.

Remember, too, that the ducks will obtain an aerial view of your vehicle and be guided accordingly. Two hundred yards on the ground seems like a long distance, particularly if you are carrying a gun and a dozen decoys; but from the air this separation of car and blind is only a few wing beats.

In the brief lull, which will probably follow the setting of the decoys, let's deal with your gunning bag.

Any kind of small bag with a shoulder strap will do, but it should have a cover to keep out the rain. I have an army surplus one which is ideal: it has compartments in it and a fold over and snap top. No zippers please—a freezing rain is only one reason against them.

What is in the bag?

A pair of 8 x 30 glasses—or a pair of substantially that power and field. Glasses add immeasurably to the pleasure of gunning, and to me they are a must. Not only do they assist you in identifying that irritating non-moving flock of ducks sitting on the water, four hundred yards away, but they are of great use in retrieving ducks.

Suppose you take a fifty-yard shot at a lone bluebill and he goes into a long glide and lands with a splash in the waves two hundred yards out. Do you take the boat and go after him, or not? If he still has plenty of vitality, he will be able to swim faster than you can row—even if he cannot fly. Further, if you go plunging around in your body of water, rowing the boat after

FIGURE 51 *Contents of gunning bag. Shells, casting line, flashlight, duck call, binoculars, rubber gloves, pocket warmer and chocolate.*

him, you are delaying your own shooting and spoiling it for anyone else left in the blind, as well as for others who may have blinds up or down the shore.

He is now, perhaps, three hundred yards away, and you see him only intermittently between the waves.

Put the glasses on him. You should have done that before. Is his head up, or is it down? If it is up, say a little prayer for him and apologize to the Great Spirit for having wounded one of his creatures. Stay in the blind and don't try to pursue him. You will be wasting your and everyone else's time. If his head is down, and the wind is blowing from you to him, go out in the boat and get him. You will probably find him dead. But take your gun along. He might make one final and desperate effort to live. If he should move when you get to within about thirty yards of him, let him have a charge of shot. He might still have the energy to dive and grab weeds. Don't shoot him from too close a range, or he won't be worth picking up. However, if you *have* to do this—in the event that he should show no signs of life until you are within five or ten yards of him—aim six or eight inches off his head so that you will not blow him to pieces.

Once, thigh deep in water, I shot twelve times at a canvasback (about ten yards away from me and over my boots) who was wounded and whose head was stretched out on the water. From time to time he would try to dive, and I could not risk letting him drift slowly in to me on the light wind. Finally a few marginal shots in the pattern caught him in the head, and I retrieved him. His body had but two shot holes in it, and he made a marvelous dinner.

Back to the gunning bag again:

Next comes the duck call—if you think that you are proficient enough with it—if not, leave it home. I usually carry a crow call, too, for the duller moments. I'm not very good at it; but sometimes a crow will come over to find out what gave grandpop the hiccups.

Extra shells—over and above the twenty-five in the belt.

I keep them loose in the bag so that I don't have to fight those self-locking pasteboard boxes with numbed fingers.

Semi-sweet or milk chocolate. It has quick energy and seems to warm you up a bit on a cold day.

If you want to be luxurious—a thermos of coffee or cocoa or soup. If you plan to stay out a good part of the day, of course, bring these and some lunch. If, however, you intend to quit at about nine o'clock, as we do, you may find all these additional groceries more or less of a nuisance and a distraction from the main job.

A casting line: This consists of the mushroom type decoy anchor (described in an earlier chapter) fastened to about thirty or forty feet of cod line, which is wound around the staff of the anchor. Put a good-sized, nonslipping loop in the free end to hold over your middle finger, so that you don't throw the whole works away in a moment of enthusiasm.

As soon as you get into the blind, put the casting line in your pocket, else you may forget to take it with you at the moment of need. If you are out, nearly tail deep in the water, trying to retrieve a duck or an escaping decoy, the casting line will do you no nourishment if it is back in the shelf in the blind.

I shall probably offend what I hope is only a small minority of gunners when I say, *Don't mix liquor and guns.*

I'm no prohibitionist. I welcome a drink, or two, or three, after five o'clock in the afternoon, with a beatific smile and the extended right hand of Bacchus. But liquor is downright dangerous in a gunning blind or at any time when you are going to use a gun.

The charge of a shotgun at short range will blow a hole in a man as big as your fist, and it's not a clean-cut wound such as would be made by a rifle ball.

Liquor puts our inner censors and watchdogs to sleep, and we are apt to become careless, overconfident and reckless. That's why most of us like to drink. None of these liquor-induced attributes are good with firearms.

Don't mix 'em.

If your blind has a shelf across the inside of the front, as it should have, put the accessories which you will need upon it —unless it is raining. If you are very fancy, of course, you can install a small roof over the shelf. Pitch the roof toward the outside of the blind.

Get comfortable. I usually carry an old piece of canvas, or discarded waterproof pants, to put on the seat to keep my tail warm and dry. Speaking of tails—if you are going to be out in the blind for a long time or are going to have to sit on beer cases in a movable blind, don't be too proud to carry one of those thin, oilcloth-covered cushions with you. Tie it to your gunning bag. It will prove to be a most efficacious prophylaxis against that occupational disease known as "blind tail."

When birds come in sight, don't point or nudge your gunning companion. Don't do what a woman I knew used to do —i.e., grab her partner by the arm, in a drowning woman's grip, so that he could not possibly raise his gun.

Don't move.

Counting a line running out into the water, at right angles to the front of the blind, as twelve o'clock, the right side of the blind as three o'clock and the left side as nine o'clock, just say quietly,

"Hold it. Three ducks at half past one, in the air." Or, if they are in the water, say so.

Thus your partner will not have to scan the hundred and eighty degrees of the horizon, like a high-power radar, to find out where the ducks are.

If you think that your face may be visible to the ducks, bend slowly forward so that it is concealed by the dressing at the front of the blind.

Don't move suddenly.

Movement—particularly of the face and hands, if they are bare—probably frightens away more ducks than any other one mistake perpetrated in the gunning blind.

Have you ever noticed, when walking through the woods, or even when driving along a road in a car, that the eye will catch the motion of even the smallest variety of bird at a considerable distance? This is because the retina of the eye is particularly sensitive to motion of any kind. I suppose that, if this were not so, the world would be inhabited by blind slugs lying on the bottom of the ocean; because any attempts to evolve higher forms would probably have ended in a free lunch for something else.

The duck, presumably, sees better than we do. This may not be so; but just observe at what a long distance you can frighten ducks off the water by lifting your arm or by merely walking along the beach. However, if you are absolutely motionless, they do not seem to be able to differentiate you from your background. I had a good example of this one time.

Several years ago, I was in a blind on a narrow cove with two friends of mine. For two hours we had watched four black ducks feeding near the opposite shore, some four hundred yards away. Finally we decided to call it quits and my two companions got out of the blind and started to get in the decoys with a long casting line. I was standing up in the blind, unloading my gun to go to help them, when the Blacks, alarmed by our movements, took to the air. I can only assume that one of the Blacks had not seen us and began to fly only because he was startled by the others. In any event, he flew straight toward us and I yelled "Freeze" and reloaded my gun. None of us moved a muscle, and in spite of the fact that we must have stood out like three Woolworth buildings on the shore, the Black came straight in and I dropped him at about thirty yards.

So many times I have seen ducks headed straight for the stool until someone in the blind lifted his head and the flash of white of his face showed through or over the blind dressing. I have often wondered whether, if one darkened one's face, one wouldn't get more shots at ducks. I plan to try it sometime.

A friend of mine, who quite frequently flies his plane between New York and this part of the world, told me, after such a trip in early November, shortly after the gunning season had opened, that the shores of Long Island Sound looked like a daisy field with all the white faces of the gunners peering up at him as he passed. And he was flying at over a thousand feet—not at two hundred.

I mentioned a casting line a few paragraphs back. At a blind, where the water is deep close in and you have to set the decoys with a boat, it will save you a great deal of time, effort and trouble if you keep an extra long casting line in the blind to retrieve the decoys and it will spare you from having to go out in the boat for them. This rig consists of the same mushroom decoy anchor, referred to previously, and about seventy-five feet of cod line. Put a small billet of wood on the free end, in case the whole works gets away from you.

Don't try to cast while standing in the water. You will not be able to get any distance.

Coil the line, on the shore next to the water, starting with the billet end so that the line will run freely. Then, after you are sure that there is no one behind you to get clipped in the jaw, whirl the anchor clockwise in the vertical plane with a length of line which allows the anchor to clear the ground by about a foot. The coiled line is, of course, in front of you, else it will tangle on your feet.

When you can feel the centrifugal force pulling hard on your hand, let the line go just after the anchor has left its nearest approach to the ground.

With very little practice you can make astonishing casts and save yourself a lot of work.

SAFETY AND MANNERS

Always look through a gun before you load it, unless you've just shot it. Snow, mud, or sand, lodged in the barrel, will likely cause a burst, with injury probably both to you and to your companions.

For reasons which are obvious, don't leave loaded guns leaning in precarious positions against a blind. As I have said before, *never forget that your gun is always cocked.*

We usually make it a practice not to load any guns until after the stool is set and we are all in the blind.

If you must leave your gun for a moment when it is loaded, stand it in a corner where it cannot fall over, and announce to your companions that it is loaded.

Don't shoot across your companions in a blind unless they tell you to and thus expect you to do it. It is a bad idea anyway; but, if their guns are empty and a cripple is getting away, they can drop back and ask you to take a whack at him.

The best way to hold a gun, when seated in a blind, is across the thighs, pointed down toward the front of the blind, and, naturally, slightly inclined to the left. Don't balance your gun, trigger guard down, with the muzzle on the front wall of the blind and the toe of the stock on the seat. It is unstable in this position and can fall over. I don't believe in this position even with the trigger guard pointed up. It may be safe enough; but when the ducks come in, you are going to have to lift your gun above the level of the blind dressing in order to get it to your shoulder—unless the blind is overly deep. This may scare the incoming ducks. From the across-the-thighs position, you can put up your gun without waving it to warn the ducks.

It is common sense, as well as common courtesy, that the right hand man take the right hand shots and vice-versa. If he misses, or causes a cripple, he should get out of the way and ask the other fellow to wipe his eye, unless the bird is too far around on the side of him who shot first. In any event, I don't believe in shooting on my companion's side at an angle of more than forty-five degrees from the twelve-o'clock line. In addition to being dangerous, it is hard on the eardrums.

If two birds come in, each gunner should shoot at the bird on his side. If more than two come in, the same rule generally applies. However, suppose seven birds are flying across the stool from left to right. The right hand man takes the lead bird, of course; but the left hand man should not shoot at the last bird. He should shoot at the third or fourth from the left; because, if he underleads, he has a chance of knocking down, with the tail end of his shot string, the bird immediately following the one he shot at.

Above all, if a big snarl of ducks comes in, don't just shoot at the flock. I know it is confusing to pick one bird out of the mass of whirring wings in front of you, but make yourself do it. If you don't train yourself to do this, the flock will, most likely, be just as large going away as it was coming in.

Speaking of large flocks of ducks, if you are gunning in a small body of water, with others near by, and you find on

FIGURE 52 *Don't hold the guns this way in a blind.*

FIGURE 53 *Man in foreground has turned gun to better position—but it still is not good.*

FIGURE 54 *This is the best way to hold guns. See text.*

your body of water a large flock of ducks, I think it is unwise to shoot at them—or perhaps even to shoot at all when they are near you. The reason for this is that the ducks may abandon your pond or bay—even if there is good feed in it—for another convenient body of water. It is preferable to induce the flock of ducks to fly out of the pond or bay and then shoot at them as they come back in small groups. Thus, the main flock will not be too deeply alarmed and you may, if you work it right, get a couple of days' shooting out of such a situation.

You may be able to scare them out by waving a coat on the shore, or, if that does not budge them, you can—as I read the federal law—go out in a rowboat. You may not, according to federal regulations, use a power boat, a sailboat, or an outboard motor. It is also illegal to use an automobile along the shore for the purpose of driving or rallying ducks.

In my remarks concerning field glasses or binoculars in the earlier part of this chapter, I mentioned the hypothetical case of a wounded bluebill who lands far out. That is just one example of how to deal with the problem of the cripple, or crope, as we call him in these parts.

Suppose a single swings in over your decoys and you drop him out of the air with the first barrel. Let us say that he hits the water thirty or forty yards out and dives.

Don't stay in the blind unless other birds are coming in near by. Don't stay in the blind if his head is up. Get out of the blind and wade as close to him as you can. I don't mean, of course, that if he is close in, you should not shoot at him again. You should. But if he is at any distance (say over thirty yards), get within a reasonable range of him if you can.

A duck, crippled or not, sitting on the water forty yards away, or even thirty, is very difficult to kill. In the first place, the heavy primary and secondary feathers on his wings protect his sides to a considerable degree, particularly against light shot. His cartilaginous back is curved like a bowl upside down upon the water, thus the pellets make contact with it at a very acute angle and can ricochet off him. This is one reason for keeping some 2 shells in the belt. His head is probably the only truly vulnerable spot at any range much over forty yards.

The fore and aft cross section of the head of a good sized black duck is probably less than four square inches and the cross section, when he is going away from you—as cripples usually are—is even less. If you have one of your old pattern targets lying about (one made at forty yards, of course), take a circular piece of paper, with a diameter of between two and two and one half inches, and place it on the target. You may be surprised at the number of places in which the circle may be lodged without touching a pellet hole.

If you want to go further into the problem, some rainy, out-of-season afternoon, make a simple silhouette of a medium-sized duck cut off at the water line and put that on your pattern target. It will serve as a practical demonstration of why the proverbial sitting duck is so hard to kill at long range.

So get as close to your waterbound cripple as you can.

If he dives, let him have it again the moment he comes up. If you do this he will not be able to get much air, before he goes down again, and will have to come up to breathe all the sooner. Meanwhile, keep walking toward him to the limit permitted by the height of your boots.

Some may find the next few paragraphs unpleasant. To me, it is extreme cruelty to drag a fluttering duck from the water, dump him on the ground outside the blind and permit him to die by degrees. I have seen ducks—particularly of the bay, sea and diving variety—tossed outside of the blind on the assumption that they were dead. I have seen them come to life again and attempt to crawl away two hours later. Unless all muscular tension has departed from the duck, he may revive and you cannot be absolutely sure, even then, that he is dead.

What is the best and most merciful way to kill a wounded duck with your hands?

Some people grab the duck by the head and whirl him around like a watchman's rattle. To my mind this method is neither merciful nor particularly effective; and if the head comes off, it makes a gory mess and it is troublesome to carry the blood-dripping duck home.

Ducks can be hand killed quickly and very mercifully as follows:

With both hands grasp the duck by the shoulders, belly up and with his head away from you. A small stone, a log, the edge of the blind, or the bow of the boat will make a suitable anvil. Swing the duck up over your shoulder and bring the back of his head down smartly upon the anvil which you have chosen. You don't have to do it very hard; if you do, you'll smash the head open and make a mess. The head and neck of the duck, plus the length of your arms, add up to a sort of snap-the-whip effect and even if the first blow does not kill the duck, it will at least render him unconscious and end his suffering. The second or third blow then can end his life.

It is an unpleasant proceeding, I know. But *you* wounded the duck, and it's up to you to finish the job humanely.

Don't be a seventh-inning gunner.

I know some people who are good shots, experienced gunners and all around charming fellows to go duck hunting with, except for one really pernicious habit. They become imbued with the idea that the seventh inning occurs about six times every hour and they get itchy-tail and have to stand up. Thereupon—in about one out of three stand-ups—a small snarl of ducks tries to visit your stool and, of course, flares off when they are some four gunshots away.

This can become a habit most irritating to your companions, and I urge you not to acquire it.

The less movement in a blind, the better. Get into the most comfortable position you can and relax everything except your eyes and your attention.

In a gunning blind, each gunner should be responsible for watching ducks on his side. Don't go into a trance and gaze out over the water to the right side of the blind when you are sitting on the left side. If you do, the ducks will almost surely sneak up on your left, out of your field of vision; you will not observe them until they pass the twelve-o'clock line and by the time you get your gun up, it will be too late for you to shoot because they will have passed too far over on your companion's side. He, in the meantime, will not have been apprised of the arrival of your feathered friends and, although he may be quick enough to throw a long-range tail shot to his extreme right, the chances are that he will not have time to shoot at all and profanity will be his only relief.

This situation often arises in the following way:

Let us say that your companion on your right remarks, "Hold it. Six ducks in the air at two o'clock." Don't snap your head around quickly and gaze at them fixedly. Bend forward, so that your face won't show, turn slowly, look at them for a moment, so that, if they do come in, you will have a general idea of the angle of their arrival, *and then resume your observation of the side which is your responsibility.*

If you don't do this, you are leaving your side unguarded and something may sneak in only to be observed too late.

This unfortunate situation may also occur in the following manner:

You observe a small snarl of ducks flying at right angles to the twelve-o'clock line, but well out of gunshot. This you announce to your partner.

When they cross that hypothetical twelve-o'clock line, however, turn them over to your companion and swing your visual radar back to your own side again, else you may miss something.

One flight of ducks is frequently followed by another, or even two or three flights, along generally the same course. Thus, if your eyes are following the caboose of the first section, you may miss seeing the second section until it is too late to shoot.

I wish I had a dollar for every time I have committed this basic error.

DOGS

A well-trained dog will spare you some of the more onerous tasks of duck hunting. If, however, you have a poorly trained or untrained dog and insufficient gunning time to train some of the fundamentals into him, you had better leave him at home under the stove, for he can be more trouble than he is worth, and your gunning expedition will probably degenerate into either a nursery school for the dog or a remedial course in dog gunning manners.

First, let me say that I have never owned a gunning dog myself; but I have shot with many dogs owned by others. Thus I perhaps have toward dogs the attitude which is held by the bachelor uncle toward his nieces and nephews. It is an attitude of skeptical tolerance mixed with a deal of ignorance.

Were I acquiring a dog for duck hunting, I think that I would pick, as number one, the golden retriever. He is intelligent, rugged and usually has a charming and affectionate personality. Next, I would select the Labrador retriever, who according to my somewhat limited experience, is nearly as good.

The Chesapeake is, of course, a wonderful duck dog; but I have met too many with dispositions which left considerable to be desired, particularly with respect to their antagonistic attitude toward other dogs.

The springer makes an acceptable gunning dog and he has a pleasant, albeit somewhat lugubrious, personality. We find that up here, this far north, the cold is a little hard on him because he is so susceptible to rheumatism. Thus, in these parts, one is liable to get only a few years' service out of him.

I have heard of Little River duck dogs—a Canadian breed—but have never shot with one. I understand that they can be trained to "toll" ducks or entice them into shore. This is a modern adaptation of the old English method, used hundreds of years ago, of attracting ducks into a large funnel-shaped duck

FIGURE 55 *The best way to scare the ducks away. Everybody looking up and giving the ducks ample warning that this is an unhealthy place. (Dressing on blind is incomplete.)*

FIGURE 56 *A pair coming in at 12 o'clock. Gunners rose to their feet at the same time. Man on right is taking bird to his left. Other two men taking bird to their right.*

trap by training a dog to run back and forth across the wide end of the funnel. The modern method seems more sporting. The ancient method seems to me one step less sporting than the Japanese procedure of scooping ducks out of the air with long-handled nets.

But back to dogs.

The dog should be trained to respond to a whistle. You'll shout yourself hoarse if he is not. Second—and this is more difficult—he should understand arm signals. Third—and perhaps most difficult of all—he should have sufficient self-restraint to remain in the blind after the guns go off and not to leave to retrieve the duck until ordered to do so.

I have had many days of what might have been good gunning spoiled by a benign old springer, who invariably burst from the blind when the ducks were about fifty yards away. Worse yet, when the ducks flared and I missed them with both barrels at this unreliable range, old Oscar would return to the blind and wither me with a look of the most utter canine scorn. He almost had me believing that it was all my fault. It was really most disconcerting.

Incidentally, the dog is, perhaps, most useful in pothole hunting where you have no boat and where the ducks may fall and be lost in thick brush.

WAVING DUCKS IN

Ever since I was very young, I have heard about waving in ducks. It is supposed to work, in general, in the same manner as tolling with dogs.

The scaup is said to be the most susceptible to this kind of blandishment. Don't try it on a black duck. He or she will immediately start for the next county.

I have tried it many times, but frankly I have never once had any success with it. However, if you want to try the method, here is the procedure which I have watched the old-timers follow:

Tie a red or yellow handkerchief to a stick about three

feet long, crawl down through the bushes as close to the shore as possible and wave your flag up and down slowly, making it disappear between each wave. If there are no bushes to conceal you, wave the flag out the side door of the blind. Keep it near the ground. If you wave it over the front of the blind it seems to frighten the ducks rather than pique their curiosity.

I have watched ducks through the glasses while the waving stunt was attempted. I have seen them lift their heads and turn toward the flag; but I have never seen them come in to it.

I know that the trick worked years ago because veracious old-timers have told me that it did. But there were more ducks then and not so many gunners. These factors may render our modern ducks more suspicious.

chapter ten

THE DAMN FOOL THINGS

Duck hunting is probably the most complicated and complex kind of hunting. It enjoys this distinction at least from the point of view, as I have said before, of the variety and amount of gear which is necessary to carry it on successfully.

The savage with a bow, five arrows and a breech clout was limited in the number of errors which he could make. He could flub his shot at his quarry, he could break his bow and he could lose his arrows or his breech clout, or both. But that was about the limit of the Damn Fool Things he could do—outside of getting lost or breaking a leg.

We, however, with our galaxies of gadgets are presented with almost infinite opportunities to misuse them and thus perpetrate a variety of the Damn Fool Things.

One of the most usual of these is the gun with the spent shells in it—or no shells at all.

You and your companion have knocked down and presumably killed a duck. There is a spanking offshore breeze and you both scramble for the boat, rip off the camouflage, launch it and start out into the great unknown—for by now the waves conceal your duck.

If you, or your companion (preferably the one who does not row) does not take a gun along, that would constitute a

Damn Fool Thing. Let's say that you don't commit this one this time, and let's say that you do the rowing and your companion takes along a gun. Coming back against the wind, you have a spirited quarter-mile row, with much grunting and some swearing, but you've picked up a magnificent red-leg black duck and the whole world is a charming, delightful and very worthwhile place.

No sooner are you back in the blind again than a pair of gregarious bluebills sweep over the stool. You are in perfect form this morning. You can't miss 'em. Up comes the gun—face firm against the stock—no barrel to be seen—lead the left one three or four feet. The safety isn't on, and you try to throw it off. Careless? No. The gun isn't loaded. You close down on the front trigger. Nothing happens. Not even a click. You break the gun, and there are the dented primers staring wide-eyed at you. You stare wild-eyed in return.

Yes, it was a Damn Fool Thing.

It is a bitter, late November morning. The wind is north-northwest and, if there were no wind, there would be ice on the water, for the temperature is well below freezing. It is dark when you arrive at the blind.

You have turned down your boots so that driving the car would be easier. In a state of partial mental confusion, compounded from having stayed up a little too late the night before, from the cold and from the buffeting of the boisterous wind, you grab two strings of decoys and start to wade out into the water.

A yell of agony. You have stepped into a small hole in the bottom and the water, which is so cold that it burns you, gushes into your turned down boots.

I've done it myself, and it's a Damn Fool Thing.

Back when it was not illegal in our Commonwealth to "possess" (at a time other than during the open season on deer) any shotgun shell containing shot larger than 2's, I used to carry a few 0-0 Buckshot or BB shells, on the remote chance that I might be able to finish off some slightly crippled duck beyond the 60-70 yard maximum effective range of the smaller shot. Incidentally, I have never succeeded in hitting a duck with 0-0 Buck.

It was not very light when I loaded my gun, which I did by taking two shells out of my gunning bag, for I had not yet been educated to appreciate the virtues of a cartridge belt.

For two hours, my companion and I watched the southern exposures of ducks proceeding in a northerly direction, a quarter of a mile or more away.

Finally our opportunity came. Three Whistlers, their music rising in pitch, headed straight into our stool. Tensely, we bent over until they were close and then on a straight incoming bird I fired first one barrel and then the other. The Whistler swung and headed for the horizon while we went out to pick up the bird which my partner had dropped.

I could not understand the miss. I knew that I had been "on" him. I knew that I had not seen barrel. Back in the blind, I was puzzling over this, when I glanced down and noticed that the two empty shells which I had removed from my gun had copper-colored heads. Then, I knew. The only copper-headed shells I owned were loaded with 0-0 Buck.

It was a Damn Fool Thing, and for two years I was referred to as Buck Shot MacKenty.

I mentioned some time back the advisability of tying a bowline or nonslipping knot in the free end of a casting line, to be slipped over the center finger of the hand tossing the weight, and fastening a billet of wood on the free end of an extra long line to be thrown by whirling. If you don't take these precautions, someday you will develop a Superman complex and chuck the whole works out into the water. And it is right at this point that your reflexes will probably play you dirt.

It is instinctive to make a grab for something you want to retain, when it is fleeing beyond your grasp. Thus, you may try to snatch at the departing end of the casting line and land in the figurative soup. Once—not, I must admit, without amusement—I watched a friend of mine grab for the departing line, lose his balance on a steep-bottomed shore, and then take a bracing sitz-bath among the ice cakes.

Speaking of ice, watch out for it. Even skim ice can trip you when you are setting decoys or retrieving a duck. Ice that is almost, but not quite, strong enough to hold you will play an even meaner and often much more dangerous trick on you. If it would only let you straight down into a foot or eighteen inches of water it might not be so bad. But it usually doesn't. What more frequently happens is that a small cake, with you on it, breaks off from the main ice, and you never find yourself standing upon its center of gravity. It tips up and slides you sideways, not too gently, and very rapidly, into the water. I have driven home quite a few shivering people who have elected to take this elementary course in dynamics.

Of course, if you walk out on doubtful ice over deep water that is more than a Damn Fool Thing. My publisher refuses to permit me to describe it adequately.

I have met ice conditions in which the ice was not strong enough to support a man standing on his feet; but would support a man sitting in a flat-bottomed boat and pushing it with his feet.

I once had to go out on ice like that after a pair of beautiful red-leg black ducks. which we had shot down and which had landed some forty or fifty yards from shore. I took a boat out on the ice and got the ducks; but let me drop two words of warning.

First, take an axe with you, lest the boat break through the ice and you have to chop a channel back to shore.

Second, take a hundred or two feet of light rope with you to the blind, when ice conditions are like this. Tie one end to the bow of the boat and have someone stand on shore with the other end, to pull you in again. Not only will this save you a lot of labor and boot soles in getting back; but if the boat does break through and you have to chop a channel, you cannot get back to shore in an offshore wind unless someone is pulling you.

It's a risky stunt under any circumstances. I guess it was a Damn Fool Thing when I did it—and probably still is.

The lighted cigarette is so commonplace that we are inclined to forget at times, how dangerous it can be. From the holocaust of forest fire to the highly personal business of burning one's self up in bed, it can cause much damage and pain. I heard of a new angle the other day.

A gunner was smoking in a blind when a pair of teal plunged into the stool. He and his companion got to their feet, the gunner dropped his cigarette—inside of his own boot—and they shot both birds. Just as the two men got back to the blind after retrieving the teal, Mr. Gunner broke into the wildest fandango ever seen on this side of the Atlantic.

It really was not too funny, however, for the lighted cigarette had lodged behind his knee near the top of his boot, where there was sufficient oxygen, and his smoldering pants and underclothes gave him quite a nasty burn.

So put your cigarette on the ground and step on it thoroughly. A cigarette dropped into a gunning bag, with shells in it, could, should its lighted end come to rest against a primer, cause a dangerous explosion.

If you are not sure of what kind of bird you have shot, don't throw it away. Take it home and compare it with the pictures in your duck book, or ask someone who is more expert than you are to identify it.

Some years ago, I went duck hunting with an avid gunner who, in spite of his interest, had had but little experience. It was a dark foggy morning and the visibility was very poor. Thus, as a case of mistaken identity—as the Who-Dun-Its say—we shot a pair of blue-billed coot. Neither of us wanted to experiment with eating them, so we did not bother to take them home.

A few days later my friend was hunting alone on one of

the blinds on my place; when we met at the house later for post-hunting coffee, we asked him what he had shot.

"Oh, just one of those damn blue-billed sea crows—like the pair we shot on Monday. I threw it in the bushes."

I was not satisfied and asked him what kind of bill and feet it had. He had not noticed the feet; but admitted that the bill was broad and more or less flattened. It was not like a crow's beak. But it was blue.

Upon my urging, he went back to his blind, and after some forty minutes of crawling through hog-brier, returned triumphantly bearing a fine fat specimen of the greater bluebill.

Even an experienced gunner makes mistakes and can shoot some innocent bird which he doesn't want to eat. Once, in a fog, I shot a dovekie at a range of some ten yards, believing that he was a duck thirty yards away.

But take home whatever you shoot, unless you are positive. It might be good to eat.

One of the Damn Fooler Things is to fail to inspect your stool, from time to time. The feathered visitor, who swims in, usually does not announce himself.

One rainy Thanksgiving Day, years ago, my daughter, a friend of mine and I were sitting huddled in a blind with the water dripping down the backs of our necks. That was before the time when I developed sense enough to put roofs on blinds, and we might as well have been sitting in a shower bath.

The weather was too miserable even for ducks and, for three hours, we had seen only a few small, distant snarls, which evinced not the slightest interest in our decoys.

I had passed the point where I thought I could smell the coffee back at the house—a mile away—and had arrived at the condition where I was sure that I could taste it. We took a vote and decided to go home.

So with casting line in hand, I got out of the blind and lumbered out into the water to start hauling in the decoys.

At this moment, out of the center of the stool there flew

a large bluebill. When he had arrived and for how long he had been there we never knew.

It was a Damn Food Thing not to have checked the decoys every few minutes or so. It almost spoiled Thanksgiving Day.

I referred earlier in this volume to pothole shooting. That is also a fertile field for the Damn Fool Things.

One of the most common errors—really an inexcusable one—involves the lack of correct timing when a group of gunners plan to converge on a pothole. I have gone into this question before; but I want to repeat, don't try to guess the time it will take Joe to get up on that hill behind those pitch pines. Synchronize your watches or at least urge your companions to measure the time in actual minutes, not by how long it takes to smoke a cigarette or to tell the latest purple story gleaned from a stockbroker friend.

One day I took five men to my favorite pothole, with which they all were more or less familiar. The fellow selected as the "scarer-outer"— a piece of bad judgment on my part— was a charming gunning companion, but possessed only a nebulous grasp of the concept of time. Instead of waiting five minutes before entering the swamp, he waited two minutes and twelve big black ducks sailed off over terrain which was not graced by any receptive gunners. They had not got halfway to their posts.

A few days later I pulled A Damn Fool Thing by waiting with the "scarer-outer" to be sure that he didn't go down into the swamp too soon. My post was only about a hundred and fifty yards away; but, since it was on a water course, it should have been occupied first, lest any of the other gunners, seeking their posts around the swamp, should flush out anything.

When I got to within fifty yards of my post, three fine black ducks went by, some thirty yards the other side of the post.

Don't take a rifle, or a pistol, or revolver into the blind with you.

According to the federal regulations, which will be dealt with briefly in the next chapter, migratory game birds may be taken *only* with a bow and arrow, or a shotgun not larger than 10-gauge. Thus, it would be a violation of the regulations to shoot, or to shoot at, ducks with a rifle, pistol or revolver. Furthermore, it is a dangerous practice.

Even the lowly .22 rifle with the Long Rifle cartridge is dangerous at a mile and the bullet will ricochet along the water for the better part of half that distance. How do you know that some gunner isn't standing in the bushes on the opposite shore? You can be quite sure that only the ducks would applaud, if you drilled a hole in him.

You just want to take the rifle along for "plinking" in case the ducks are not flying today? Don't do it. Temptation might overcome you. You might take just one shot to stir up that small flock sitting on the water, a quarter of a mile away.

It would be bad enough to have the long arm of the Law grab you; but it would be far worse should you maim or kill some other gunner.

It is not worth the risk.

If you own, or someone in your family owns, a 16-gauge gun and you use a 12-gauge on ducks, take an extra look-see at that box of shells or the cartridge belt which you pick up in the dark hall at five A. M. You may save yourself a disagreeable surprise when you get into your blind.

Many years ago, when I was still shooting the old 10-bore, I traveled a long way to a blind and did not notice until I came to loading my gun that I had brought along a belt full of 12-gauge shells.

It was a long and profane round trip, from blind to house and from house to blind.

If anyone is shooting a 20-gauge next to a 12-gauge or a 10-gauge, just remember that a 20-gauge shell will drop into the 12-gauge or the 10-gauge barrel below the limits of the chamber so that the correct shell can be inserted behind it. The 16-gauge shell will also drop below the chamber of a 10-gauge gun and lodge in the barrel. The 28-gauge will do the same in the 20-gauge gun.

A Mills hand grenade exploding in the blind would probably be no more lethal in its effects than the pieces of the plugged gun under such circumstances.

One day, a long time ago, I took a charming lady gunning with me. She had never seen a duck shot, had never shot a gun herself, didn't plan to, and really just came along for the ride. It was early in the season and a warm bluebirdish day.

For the first hour or so, she burbled happily about the beauties of the sunrise and the soaring gulls, and no ducks came near us.

Finally, a lone bufflehead came flying up the cove at such long range that, under normal circumstances, I don't think I would have considered trying a shot at him. However, I had to risk my mediocre reputation as a shot in order to save the reputation of my shore land as a place for ducks.

I led him about ten feet and, by pure good luck, hit him. He struck the water and bounced twice, like a skipping stone. The glasses showed that his head was under.

When I retrieved him, and bore him proudly back to the lady, I noticed that but one pellet had hit him—and in the eye. The lady looked him over with mixed emotions of repugnance and curiosity and then exclaimed, "What a wonderful shot. You hit him *right* in the eye!"

I tried to explain the difference between a shotgun and a rifle, but it was no use. I'd hit him in the eye. Of course, it was a marvelous shot. I was just being modest.

The reputation thus unjustly acquired embarrassed me with my gunning friends for a long time.

There is always charm in the unexpected—unless it is unpleasant—and one of the basic attractions of duck hunting is the frequent incidence of the unforeseen. However, the unexpected in duck hunting seems to be perverse. It almost always occurs at the most inopportune moments:

When you and your companion are in the boat a quarter of a mile out from shore, chasing a cripple, erroneously assumed to be dead, because you were in too much of a hurry to look at him through your glasses—

When you are setting out the decoys and the soft, pink fingers of dawn are clutching at the eastern sky—

When skunked and disgusted and nearly tail deep in the water picking up the decoys preparatory to going home—

When the decoys are neatly lined up on the shore, when the guns are unloaded and sheathed in their cases and you are leaving the gunning site—

It is at one or more of these times that the snarl of twenty bluebills tries to knock off the roof of the blind.

chapter eleven

CONSERVATION AND THE LAW

Too many gunners, I fear, look upon game wardens and conservation officers as kill-joys appointed especially to deprive the gunner of a large part of the joys of hunting ducks. Actually, these men are endeavoring only to enforce laws and regulations, in the formulation of which they have played little or no part.

The federal regulations, which will be dealt with broadly a little later, have been devised in good faith to secure the greatest good for the greatest number of people. Thus, even if certain of these regulations appear to you to be illogical, I think that you should, nevertheless, adhere to them, if only for the sake of the good example which your so doing creates.

Don't be irritated and surly if a warden or conservation officer requests you to show your license or duck stamp. This is one of his duties and he is merely performing them and is not trying to be officious.

We should remember that, were it not for the existence of the federal regulations and the state laws governing the "taking" of water fowl, such as the establishment of duration of open season and size of bag, there would probably be no duck hunting in this country today. We should, therefore, support and conform to these regulations and laws as closely as possible, so that we, and those who will come after us, may enjoy this grand old sport.

It is not many decades since spring shooting was in existence, and I can remember market gunning when I was a youngster. Many of us can recollect the day in which game was sold in butchershops, and the horse-drawn delivery vans carried, on each side, a pair of stuffed mallards or canvasbacks protected by glass covers.

The regulations and laws came almost too late, perhaps a decade or two too late; but they have saved some gunning for us and, with the aid of the good work being carried forward by that excellent organization, Ducks Unlimited, there are more ducks today than there were ten years ago.

When grousing about shortened seasons and small bag limits, just stop and remember the fate of the shore birds—the plovers, the snipe, the stilts, the godwits, the sanderlings.

Less than fifty years ago, there were literally millions of these upon our shores. Their intelligence and their abilities toward self-preservation are less than those of the duck tribe, and protection and conservation came too late to save them. They are rare in New England, and there is now no open season on them. Only the ghosts of the hordes of those which lived—not too long ago—flit over the tidal mud flats, the sand dunes and the beach grasses.

I shall not attempt, in these pages, to deal with the state game laws. They would occupy a whole book in themselves and besides many of them are modified from year to year.

In a very general way, I shall outline some of the more important aspects of the federal regulations; but remember that alterations are made in these every year and you should obtain a copy of the new regulations each year, together with a copy of the laws of the state in which you hunt—and be guided accordingly.

Ducks and geese, as I have mentioned before, may be "taken" only with a bow and arrow or with a shotgun not larger than a 10-gauge. The latter must be fired from the shoulder.*

Automatic shotguns and hand-operated repeating guns, holding more than three shells, including the shell in the chamber, must be plugged so that they will not hold more than three shells, counting the one in the chamber. Such plug shall be incapable of removal without disassembling the gun.

"Take," incidentally, is defined as, "hunt, kill or capture, or attempt to hunt, kill or capture."

Waterfowl may be taken during the open season established each year for each state, from the land or the water, with the aid of a dog, and from a blind, boat, or other floating craft not under tow or sail, but not from a sinkbox (or battery) or from a motorboat (not including a boat having a detached outboard motor) or from a sailboat unless such motorboat or sailboat is fastened within or tied immediately alongside of any type of stationary hunting blind. It is not permitted to take waterfowl by means, aid, or use of any motor-driven conveyance, motor vehicle or aircraft or by means, aid or use of cattle, horses, mules or live duck or goose decoys. It is also not permitted to concentrate, drive, rally or stir up waterfowl by means or aid of any motor-driven land, water, or air conveyance or sailboat. But you are permitted to pick up dead or injured waterfowl by means of a motorboat, sailboat or other craft.

You may not take waterfowl within half a mile of any place where birds have been fed within two weeks prior to the open season. Furthermore, waterfowl may not be taken with the aid of feed put out to entice them to the area where hunters are attempting to take them.† Standing crops on land, or grain

* This provision, presumably, is designed to rule out the old punt guns of the market gunning days. This was a sort of small cannon mounted on a swivel in the bow of a boat. It was employed to shoot into flocks of ducks sitting on the water.

† I have always understood that planted feed growing in the water does not come within the scope of this prohibition.

scattered as a result of normal agricultural harvesting, are not included in this prohibition; nor is it forbidden to feed waterfowl at any time not in connection with hunting.

Each person over sixteen years of age must have in his or her possession a duck stamp at the time of taking waterfowl. Such stamp must have such person's signature written across the face thereof. Persons under sixteen years of age do not have to possess such a stamp.

The hours for taking waterfowl during the open seasons extend from a half an hour before sunrise to one hour before sunset. Perhaps I might as well comment on this phase of the Regulations, right here.

Any law is only as strong, in its capacity to be observed, as its least enforceable provision. In other words, the flouting of one provision of a Law—because of its impracticality or unpopularity or unenforceability—weakens all the provisions not only of that law but of all other laws as well. If a man violates one provision of a law with impunity, he will be inclined to evade other provisions or other laws. Vide, the Prohibition Amendment to the Constitution and the Volstead Act.

Now, on a dull overcast morning, when it's either spitting rain or threatening to, and the clouds and scud are lowering over the trees or dunes, a half an hour before sunrise is probably about the earliest time you can see to shoot, anyway. But, if you are sitting under a pale azure and cloudless sky, tinged on the east with the pink of impending sunrise, you can see well enough to shoot at forty-five to sixty minutes before sunrise. At this juncture and hour, a pair of scaup or black ducks plop into the stool; and what does Mr. Average Gunner do? I doubt that you require more than one guess.

The regrettable part of this act is not that a few ducks have been taken before the legal hour. It is that Mr. Average Gunner has, by his own deed, reduced his own and his companions' respect for the law. Having committed one violation, it is now easier—that is, easier on the conscience—to violate, for example, the bag limit.

Why not permit shooting forty-five minutes before sunrise? I believe that the half hour before sunrise regulation came in when the now banned sinkbox or battery was legal. This starting hour does not fit in well with blind shooting.

As to the hour-before-sunset regulation, I think that this is even worse.

We all have observed that ducks do not move about much in the middle of the day. Here, we usually pull in the decoys by nine or nine thirty, in the morning. In this latitude, in early December, the sun sets shortly after four o'clock. This means that it is not legal to hunt later than a few minutes past three and, what it means, as a practical matter, is that legal afternoon shooting is out.

Let's not use the second person plural pronoun but, instead, bring Mr. Average Gunner on the stage again.

By employing all his powers of persuasion, Mr. Average Gunner (we'll call him Avy in order to save ink) has talked his boss into letting him have a day off to go gunning, and Avy has taken his best girl's father hunting, for reasons which are obvious and need not be dealt with here. The old man has been gunning for forty years—and still loves it.

It's a bluebird day, the ducks have rafted up in the wide waters and won't fly. By two thirty they are still skunked and the curfew will ring at three fifteen.

At three, a small snarl of ducks tears itself from the main raft a mile away, swings around the bay and settles down about a hundred and fifty yards outside the stool. Both Avy and the man who he hopes will become his father-in-law are crouched, bent over, tense and motionless, in the blind.

The minutes tick by. The ducks swim in a little ways and then they swim out a little ways. Proposed father-in-law's blood pressure is getting dangerously high. Avy is thinking of his rash promise to the old man that they would have their limit by nine o'clock.

Figuratively speaking, the curfew rings; but there is no one within a mile or two of Avy and his companion. The ducks are definitely closer now—much closer.

"To hell with the damn fool law! We're going to have a duck dinner. Myrtle cooks 'em swell."

At four o'clock, forty-five minutes within the illegal era, they get their duck dinner.

Now, just suppose the game warden comes along a few minutes after the dinner was procured.

"Didn't I hear you fellows shoot, about ten, fifteen minutes ago?"

"Sure. We had a hell of a time getting that cripple. Shot at him 'bout an hour ago and he swam up against the wind. Got tired, I guess, and drifted back."

No proof, no witnesses. Two words against one. The game warden may let the matter drop there. After all, he did not see them shoot.

Again, the sad part of this is not the two ducks shot: it is the disrespect for the law which has been engendered in these two otherwise honorable gunners.

The cure for this? Restore the old half an hour after sunset law, which we had here in Massachusetts. Darkness will stop the shooting and violations will be reduced. I doubt, however, that the duck population would be much reduced by such a reversion. In my experience, after the season has been open for a few days, the Blacks usually don't come into the cove heads and swamps until after dark and the bay, sea, and diving ducks are not very active around sundown.

The bag limits change from year to year, so there is no need to deal with them at length here. The bag limits also vary in different parts of the country. For example, in 1952, the Atlantic and Mississippi flyway states had a daily bag limit of four ducks and a possession limit of eight ducks. The central flyway states had a bag limit of five and a possession limit of ten. In the Pacific flyway both daily bag limit and possession were set at six,* a process of logic which has never been apparent to me. It seems strange that the daily bag limit for the Pacific flyway should have been fifty per cent higher than that applying

* The foregoing general statements are subject to several qualifications and exceptions, e.g., the limits on scoter and mergansers are larger. Also, in certain states, the open season on scoters, outside of harbor limits, is longer.

to the eastern sections of the country, while the possession limit was set at twenty-five per cent less than that established for such sections.

If you are one of those affluent gunners who can afford to hire a guide or a paid gunner to hunt with you, it is well to remember that the regulations provide that any birds shot by the hired hand count on your limit.

There is, in the regulations, a prohibition against hunting on any reservation or sanctuary.

It is also well to remember that no migratory bird may be "taken" at any time, by any means, from, on, or across any highway, road, trail, or other right of way—whether public or private—within the boundaries of any duly established national wild life refuge.

The regulations with reference to possession are quite strict and were evidently drawn without recognition of the now prevalent use of deep freezers. You may possess migratory game birds during the open season and for ninety days thereafter, not longer. There are certain new and rather stringent regulations pertaining to the storage, shipment and transfer of ducks.

There are various special provisions, of no particular interest to the duck hunter, relating to the possession of live migratory game birds and the plumage and skins thereof and to the killing, frightening, or otherwise herding of such birds, causing injury to agriculture or other interests.

The regulations close with a general denial reciting that nothing therein contained shall be construed as permitting any act contrary to the laws and regulations of any State, when such laws and regulations are not inconsistent with the conventions between the United States and any other country for the protection of migratory birds or with the Migratory Bird Treaty Act and when such state laws and regulations do not extend the open season for birds beyond the dates provided in the federal regulations.

This means that you should make yourself familiar with the laws and regulations of the state in which you hunt, because, in many instances they go beyond the limitations and restrictions imposed by the federal regulations.

Officials From Whom Copies of Game Laws May Be Obtained

FEDERAL LAWS: Secretary of the Interior, Washington 25, D. C.; Director, Fish and Wildlife Service, Department of the Interior, Washington 25, D. C.; and Regional Directors of the Fish and Wildlife Service with headquarters as follows: *Region 1* (Western), Swan Island, Portland 18, Oreg.; *Region 2* (Southwestern), 220 West Copper Avenue (P. O. Box 1306), Albuquerque, N. Mex.; *Region 3* (North Central), Buzza Building, 1006 West Lake St., Minneapolis 8, Minn.; *Region 4* (Southeastern), Peachtree-Seventh Building, Atlanta 5, Ga.; *Region 5* (Northeastern), 1105 Blake Building, Boston 11, Mass.; *Region 6,* Juneau, Alaska.

ALABAMA: Director, Division of Game, Fish and Seafoods, Department of Conservation, Montgomery 4.

ALASKA: Fish and Wildlife Service, Juneau, or Secretary of the Interior, Washington 25, D. C.

ARIZONA: Director, Game and Fish Commission, Arizona State Building, Phoenix.

ARKANSAS: Executive Secretary, Game and Fish Commission, Little Rock.

CALIFORNIA: Director, Department of Fish and Game, Ferry Building, San Francisco 11.

COLORADO: Director, Game and Fish Commission, 1530 Sherman Street, Denver 5.

CONNECTICUT: Superintendent, Board of Fisheries and Game, State Office Building, Hartford 1.

DELAWARE: Chief Warden, Board of Game and Fish Commissioners, Dover.

DISTRICT OF COLUMBIA: Superintendent, Metropolitan Police, Washington.

FLORIDA: Director, Game and Fresh Water Fish Commission, Tallahassee.

GEORGIA: Director, Game and Fish Commission, 412 State Capitol, Atlanta 3.

HAWAII: Fish and Game Division, Commissioners of Agriculture and Forestry, Honolulu.

IDAHO: Director, Department of Fish and Game, Boise.

ILLINOIS: Director, Department of Conservation, Springfield.

INDIANA: Director, Division of Fish and Game, Department of Conservation, 311 West Washington Street, Indianapolis 9.

IOWA: Director, State Conservation Commission, East Seventh and Court Streets, Des Moines.

KANSAS: Director, Forestry, Fish and Game Commission, Pratt.

KENTUCKY: Commissioner, Department of Fish and Wildlife Resources, Frankfort.

LOUISIANA: Commissioner, Department of Wild Life and Fisheries, 126 Civil Courts Building, New Orleans 16.

MAINE: Commissioner, Department of Inland Fisheries and Game, State House, Augusta.

MARYLAND: Director, Game and Inland Fish Commission, 514 Munsey Building, Baltimore 2.

MASSACHUSETTS: Director, Division of Fisheries and Game, Department of Conservation, 15 Ashburton Place, Boston 8.

MICHIGAN: Director, Department of Conservation, Lansing 13.

MINNESOTA: Commissioner, Department of Conservation, State Office Building, St. Paul 1.

MISSISSIPPI: Director, Game and Fish Commission, 330 East Pearl Street, Jackson.

MISSOURI: Director, Conservation Commission, Monroe Building, Jefferson City.

MONTANA: State Fish and Game Warden, Department of Fish and Game, Helena.

NEBRASKA: Executive Secretary, Game, Forestation and Parks Commission, Lincoln 9.

NEVADA: Director, Fish and Game Commission, Box 678, Reno.

NEW HAMPSHIRE: Director, Fish and Game Department, State House Annex, Concord.

NEW JERSEY: Director, Department of Conservation and Economic Development, State House Annex, Trenton 7.

NEW MEXICO: State Game Warden, Department of Game and Fish, Santa Fe.

NEW YORK: Commissioner, Conservation Department, Albany 7.

NORTH CAROLINA: Executive Director, Wildlife Resources Commission, Raleigh.

NORTH DAKOTA: Commissioner, Game and Fish Department, Capitol Building, Bismarck.

OHIO: Chief, Division of Wild Life, Department of Natural Resources, 1500 Dublin Road, Columbus 15.

OKLAHOMA: Director, Game and Fish Department, State Capitol Building, Room 118, Oklahoma City 5.

OREGON: State Game Director, State Game Commission, P. O. Box 4136, Portland 8.

PENNSYLVANIA: Executive Director, Pennsylvania Game Commission, Harrisburg.

PUERTO RICO: Department of Agriculture and Commerce, Division of Fisheries and Wildlife, San Juan.

RHODE ISLAND: Administrator, Division of Fish and Game, Department of Agriculture and Conservation, State House, Providence 2.

SOUTH CAROLINA: Director, Wildlife Resources Commission, Columbia.

SOUTH DAKOTA: Director, Department of Game, Fish and Parks, Pierre.

TENNESSEE: Director, Tennessee Game and Fish Commission, 166 Eighth Avenue, North, Nashville.

TEXAS: Executive Secretary, Game and Fish Commission, Austin.

UTAH: Director, Fish and Game Commission, 1596 West North Temple, Salt Lake City 16.

VERMONT: Director, Fish and Game Service, Montpelier.

VIRGINIA: Executive Director, Commission of Game and Inland Fisheries, P. O. Box 1642, Richmond 13.

WASHINGTON: Director, Department of Game, 509 Fairview Avenue, North, Seattle 9.

WEST VIRGINIA: Director, Conservation Commission of West Virginia, Charleston.

WISCONSIN: Director, Conservation Department, State Office Building, Madison 2.

WYOMING: State Game and Fish Commissioner, Wyoming Game and Fish Commission, Cheyenne.

CANADA: Chief, Canadian Wildlife Service, Department of Resources and Development, Ottawa.

ALBERTA: Fish and Game Commissioner, Department of Lands and Forests, Edmonton.

BRITISH COLUMBIA: Game Commissioner, Office of Game Commission, 567 Burrard Street, Vancouver.

MANITOBA: Director of Game and Fisheries, Winnipeg.

NEW BRUNSWICK: Chief Game Warden, Department of Lands and Mines, Fredericton.

NEWFOUNDLAND: Chief Game Warden, Department of Natural Resources, St. John's.

NORTHWEST TERRITORIES: Deputy Commissioner, Department of Resources and Development, Ottawa.

NOVA SCOTIA: Deputy Minister of Lands and Forests, Halifax.

ONTARIO: Chief, Fish and Wildlife Division, Department of Lands and Forests, Toronto 2.

PRINCE EDWARD ISLAND: Deputy Minister of Industry and Natural Resources, Charlottetown.

PROVINCE OF QUEBEC: General Superintendent, Department of Game and Fish, Quebec.

SASKATCHEWAN: Game Commissioner, Department of Natural Resources, Saskatchewan Resources Building, Regina.

YUKON TERRITORY: Commissioner, Yukon Territory, Dawson, Y. T.

MEXICO. Secretaria de Agricultura y Ganaderia, Direccion General Forestal y de Caza, México, D. F.

chapter twelve

CLEANING, COOKING AND EATING

I know many gunners who are enthusiastic hunters but who do not care to eat what they have brought down.

There's no accounting for taste, as the old lady said when she kissed the cow. Therefore, I do not deplore this lack of enthusiasm for eating ducks, except in instances in which the ducks are left hanging behind the woodshed to rot, instead of being given away to some gourmet who likes them. To have no one eat and enjoy what you have shot is wasteful and inexcusable.

There are two main methods of cleaning ducks:

1. Have the butcher do it
2. Do it yourself

As to the first, even the old-fashioned, neighborhood butcher shop is rapidly losing the art of dressing or cleaning any kind of fowl or animal. This work is done nowadays on a production-line basis by packers. Taking a dead duck in your fist into some magnificent supermarket would probably elicit the same reaction as walking into Tiffany's with a two-and-a-half-dollar alarm clock and asking them to repair it.

So the chances are that you will have to clean your ducks yourself; and here are a few suggestions:

As to defeathering, there are two principal methods for the home duck cleaner.

The brute force method consists of the time-honored way of pulling the feathers out with the thumb and forefinger, both of which get pretty tired if there are three or four ducks to clean. If ducks are plucked immediately after being shot, it is not so difficult; but usually it is inconvenient to do this; furthermore, some people believe that a duck should be hung for a couple of days in his feathers. I don't belong to this school of thought, myself, but hold the opinion that the sooner a duck is cleaned, the better. This is particularly true if any shot have punctured the intestines and especially the gall.

If you want to use the brute force method—which I do not recommend—and if you are going to do it indoors, bring your wife a dozen roses as a palliative for her forthcoming ire and get out the vacuum cleaner to suck up the feathers which will fill the room in which you work.

The brute force method is really much better out of doors.

As a first step, remove the head and neck close to the body; cut off the feet at the knee joint (that's where the feathers begin) and clip off the wing up to the first joint. This saves you the trouble of pulling out all the heavy primary feathers, which are set in very tightly. You can, if you want to conserve more effort, remove the entire wing; but, when your duck comes to table, he will be slightly reminiscent of the Venus de Milo.

If the feathers are very hard to pluck, you can dip your duck in a bucket of boiling water; but this method evokes the serious disadvantage that the wet feathers will stick to you and to everything else.

The wax method is far preferable to the brute force method. There are two ways of employing it.

If you use either of the two wax methods, probably a half-dozen roses for your wife will be sufficient, because this way of defeathering ducks engages only a small portion of the stove. Better yet, it creates very little mess.

METHOD ONE

Procure an old pan that nobody loves any more. It should be two or three inches deep, have no leaks in it, of course, and be large enough so that you can get the duck into it and still have room to hold on to him with both hands, one at each end. Procure also some cakes of wax, the kind that the gals use for sealing the tops of jam and jelly glasses. Melt enough wax in the pan so that the liquid wax stands about an inch deep, or a little more. Remember that wax has a flash point, as has any oil, and don't get it too hot or let it vaporize, particularly on a range with an open flame. You could cause a fire, although with any care the stunt is perfectly safe. Your wife can tell you how to do it.

With both wax methods, it is more convenient to leave the head and feet on to use as handles while waxing. First, cut the wings off at the elbow. Next, pull out some of the bigger feathers so the duck won't soak up too much wax, and then, holding him by head and feet, with one hand at each end, roll him over and over in the melted wax until there is a good heavy coat of wax on all the remaining feathers all over him. Set him aside—on a piece of waxed paper to cool. If the kitchen is too hot, put him out of doors for a few minutes. The wax should be allowed to get firm and entirely cooled all the way through. A good dog probably won't touch him; but don't trust the cats. Put him in a safe place.

As soon as the wax is hard, take him inside. With a good sharp knife, cut through the wax—but not through the skin, if you can help it—making the incision along or parallel to the breastbone. Starting with the knife, and using your fingers later, pry the wax and skin gently and carefully away from each other. All the feathers, including the most stubborn and elusive of the pin feathers, will come away with the wax and you can actually peel all the feathers off him in a very few minutes. It will facilitate your task if, as you progress, you make other incisions in the wax with a knife at the stubborn points, such as the legs and the loose skin under the wings.

METHOD TWO

This is similar to Method One, except that a pan of water is brought almost to the boiling point and the wax dropped into it. The pan should be a wide one so that you can insert the duck readily. Two or three inches of water is enough. Three or four 2½″ x 5″ x ½″ cakes of wax will be sufficient. The wax will melt almost immediately and, being lighter than water, will form a liquid, but usually invisible, layer on top of it. Into this you may dip the duck, covering him well with wax. Even if he gets down into the water, it won't make much difference, because he will have been waterproofed by the layer of wax on the way through, although, if you let the water touch him for too long, it will melt the wax off him again. Don't let the water boil. The rising steam will scald you and will melt the wax off the duck.

Method Two is undoubtedly the better because it is safer and because there is no pan scraping afterwards. Just let the water cool and the pieces of floating wax can be lifted off and used on other ducks.

The removal of wax and feathers is, of course, the same as in method one. Be sure to let the wax get good and hard before going to work.

DETERGENTS

I have heard of immersing the duck in a bucket of very hot water containing a few heaping tablespoonfuls of any standard kitchen dishwashing detergent and then plucking the duck by hand. This may be superior to the plain hot water method mentioned above, but it would still be subject to its drawbacks of messiness. Furthermore, I am not sure that I would like soap on my meat.

THE BUTCHERING

Put the duck on his back, and, with a sharp knife—the sharper the better—make one central incision from the center of the wishbone to the neck and another from the rear of the breastbone to the vent which should be removed along with the fleshy tail of the duck. Don't cut too deeply lest you puncture the intestines.

The plumbing, as in all fowl, should be removed from the rear or rumble-seat end. There is one trick about this which will render the somewhat unpleasant job much easier. The trachea and gullet of most ducks are attached quite securely at one point to the anterior side of the spine, just aft of where the neck enters the body of the duck. This point can be located with the fingers through the incision made from the wishbone to the neck. When you find it, cut the trachea and gullet free with a sharp knife or good scissors. After this is done, all the plumbing may be easily drawn out of the south end of the duck.

Some people do not believe in washing out the inside of a duck, after he has been drawn. I do.

As mentioned above, a stray shot pellet or two may have punctured the intestines or the gall, and the seepage from either of these will not contribute endearing flavor to the meat. Let the water from the *cold*-water faucet run through the now hollow duck and remove any odd blood clots or strips of tissue with your fingers. Be sure that you remove the lungs. They usually do not come away with the rest of the plumbing. Wrap the duck tightly in several layers of good wax paper and put him in the refrigerator.

If you plan to put the duck into a deep freezer it is better to seal him up hermetically in one of those plastic type bags, which can be procured, nowadays, almost anywhere. If you do not do this, he will tend to become dehydrated and will lose his flavor, if you keep him for any length of time.

Before proceeding to the rather simple process of cooking the duck, it might be well to deal with the semi-edible ducks—notably the mergansers and the scoters.

That rancid fish-mortuary taste which one perceives in the fish-eating ducks, of which these two species are perhaps the most common, resides in the layer of fat, with which all ducks are covered. You can, of course, skin the whole duck, removing the fat in the process, and then roast him; but, in the absence of the basting and insulating effects of his own fat, he will be very dry and unpalatable. I don't recommend this method.

The merganser can be made into a very acceptable dish by filleting off the breasts. This can be done very easily and quickly with a sharp knife.

Simply take the whole duck, head, feathers, feet and all, put him on his back and, cleaving as closely to the breastbone as possible, and beginning at the center line or peak of the breastbone, cut off each breast including the skin with the attached feathers. After the two breasts are removed, the skin and feathers may be peeled off in one motion. Don't try to skin him before you remove the breast. The skin will curl inward and get in your way.

Scrape any fragments of fat off the two fillets thus secured, and give them a critical sniff or two. If they are somewhat reminiscent of a fish, put about a pint of lukewarm water in a pan and add a teaspoonful of salt and one of baking soda (sodium bicarbonate). Let the fillets soak in this solution for fifteen or twenty minutes, take out, dry with paper towels, wrap tightly in several layers of waxed paper and put in the refrigerator until you are ready to use them.

The same process may be used in the case of the scoter, but this bird has a strong, penetrating flavor of his own, beyond the fish taste, which you may not like.

The ruddy duck constitutes, with the masked duck (not found in North America), a subfamily all to himself. From my experience with him, he is nearly as tough to pluck as a goose, which is saying a great deal. You will almost need pliers to get those spiky tail feathers out; but the wax method will simplify the remainder of the job. However, if you are plucking him by the brute force method and get discouraged, I suggest that you fillet him. His legs are so small that they are barely worth saving anyway. Leave the skin and fat on the fillets, if you can; because they will add to the flavor.

One more thing before we come to the actual cooking:

Some people prefer to hang their ducks until they are "high." I don't, because I do not like carrion. But again, that is a matter of taste.

It will make a duck more tender, I believe, if you keep him in a temperature around the lower forties for from two to four days; but, as I have mentioned before, I like to pluck and dress him as soon as practicable. If the temperature is kept close to forty, or below, you can keep him two or three days longer.

THE COOKING

There are three main schools of thought on cooking ducks:

1. The "blood should follow the knife" school
2. The "medium-rare beefsteak" school
3. The "cook 'em to death, like a Long Island duckling" school

I tolerate the first, belong to the second and refuse even to discuss the third.

The least gamey ducks—the pond and river ducks—can be cooked either with or without stuffing. The bay, sea and diving ducks are gamier and stronger in flavor and have greater need for the supplemental seasoning of stuffing. I prefer all ducks stuffed, simply because I enjoy the combination of flavors.

If you have the metabolism of a tiger—which I have not—you can eat and enjoy the stuffing; but it will be thoroughly saturated with duck grease, which has a pretty high octane rating. I stuff ducks more for the purpose of creating flavor than for the purpose of adding something particularly edible to the meal.

As with all meat, take your duck out of the refrigerator about an hour before he is to go into the fiery furnace. When he is about up to room temperature, rub him all over generously with olive oil. This will help to give him a fine sepia tone when he emerges from the oven. Don't put any salt on him.

The stuffing which I find most satisfactory and contributory in flavor is composed of roughly equal parts of cut up oranges (skins removed), onions and apples (cores but not skins removed). I cut the oranges and apples into about one-inch cubes and the onions into smaller bits, mix them together and then stuff the duck quite tightly. Next, procure a slab of fat salt pork, about a half an inch to an inch thick and cut it into as thin slices as you can, each slice being around three or four inches long. Put the duck on his back in a dry pan and cover the breast with five or six slices of the salt pork, placing the strips crosswise.

Now preheat the oven to four hundred and fifty degrees.

If you are cooking more than one duck and they vary in size, place your smaller ducks in the end of the pan nearer the oven door. If the size varies too much–say you have a large mallard and a small teal–you may have to cook your mallard for a few minutes alone, open the oven and then put in the teal.

I find that from ten to twelve minutes in the oven at four hundred and fifty degrees gives a good browning and seals in the juices of the larger and medium-sized ducks, such as mallards, the two types of blacks, greater scaup and goldeneyes. Smaller ducks, such as the teal, bufflehead and ruddy duck should be kept at this temperature for about eight or nine minutes. At the critical moment, cut the oven temperature to three hundred and fifty degrees and *vent the oven by holding the door open until it drops to that temperature.*

The larger ducks stay in the oven twenty to twenty-five minutes more at this lower temperature, the smaller ones about fifteen to twenty.

Since ducks are so hard to come by nowadays, don't spoil yours in this last step–the cooking. If you are at all doubtful about the accuracy of the thermostat in your oven, take your carving knife and, after the ducks have been in the oven for the length of time suggested above, make a lengthwise and fairly deep incision in the breast. If the meat looks like good rare beefsteak, it is done. If it has the purplish tinge of hamburger in a showcase, leave the ducks in the oven for another few minutes. There is a critical point in the gradual breakdown of the meat, caused by the heat, at which the consistency of the meat changes quite rapidly from that of bubble gum to a fibrous structure like that of properly cooked rare beef. It is just beyond this point in the progress of the cooking that the ducks should be removed from the oven and are ready to eat.

They should now be perfect for those who belong to the school of thought number two—the "medium-rare beefsteak" school. The adherents to the "blood follows the knife" school will want to reduce these times for the larger ducks to about nine minutes at four hundred and fifty degrees and ten to twelve minutes at three hundred and fifty. Little ducks should have perhaps seven or eight minutes at four hundred and fifty and may be eight or nine more at three fifty. I am not too well versed in the tenets of this school.

As to the third school—the "cook 'em to death" school—they can boil their ducks in sea water or kerosene, and see if I care.

I mentioned filleting a while ago.

If you are an addict of fireplace cookery, I think the best way to cook a filleted duck breast is to wrap it in bacon and broil it over charcoal or oak coals. Done in this way, merganser tastes a deal like venison, albeit perhaps not quite so tender.

The broiler in the stove is next in line of preference; or, if you are disinclined to use this, you can sauté the fillets in butter and a little onion in the frying pan.

Whichever method you use, don't overcook them. Take them off the fire while they still have a good rich pinkish tinge in the center.

You can try scoter this way and you may like it. I don't. It is too strong. You can, as an alternative, make him into a stew.

Here in New England this is sometimes accomplished as follows:

Skin the scoter (you won't have to pluck him), and cut him up in sizable pieces. Don't use the carcass. Employ only the wings, legs and each breast cut into four or five pieces. Sauté the pieces in butter and onion until the meat is well browned. Then place potatoes, carrots and more onions in a casserole; add the meat and the gravy from the sautéing. A little poultry seasoning will help to dull the scoter taste. You will probably need to add a little water too, and, if you like the gravy thickened, a little flour can be stirred gradually into it before it is added to the mixture. Put the covered casserole in a low oven for about two hours. Check your water content from time to time.

Finally, if the scoter flavor still comes through too strongly, add two or three ounces of Bordeaux or red Burgundy to the stew, about half an hour before serving, and stir it well.

EATING

Wild duck is an extremely rich and, to me, energy-imparting food. After eating a duck dinner, I always feel as if one or two extra highballs had, by some magic alchemy, crawled into my system. Good rare beef has, to a lesser extent, the same effect; but wild duck is triple-distilled and over-proof. It is a wonderful food.

This indicates, to my mind, that the other elements of the dinner should, with perhaps one exception, be simple and rather plain, lest other rich items on the menu compete unfavorably with the pièce de résistance. Thus, unless you and your guests have been gunning or tramping all day, or unless you are short of duck, don't serve a heavy soup, such as pea or black bean, or any cream soup. A consommé or a madrilene will be sufficient.

As for the accompanying vegetables, the only rich and heavy one which I advise is wild rice. This is, of course, rich, but it seems to be a natural companion to wild duck. Put a tablespoon of lemon juice in it when you are cooking it and don't get it overdone and soggy. One green vegetable in addition should be enough. Select one low in esters—not broccoli or cauliflower. Serve something neutral in flavor such as string beans or peas.

There are two other "must" accompaniments to your duck dinner—red currant jelly and wine.

Red currant jelly eaten with duck meat creates nuances of flavor that the duck alone cannot attain. Combined with the aura of orange, onion and baked apple, it creates what the radio announcers call a "taste sensation." It is really something to wake up in the night and think about. Have plenty of this jelly on hand.

It goes without saying that the wine should be red—preferably a Burgundy, but a good stout Bordeaux will do quite nicely.

If your pocketbook feels strong and rugged, jump off the deep end and purchase a good French wine such as Chateau Cheval Blanc, or Chateau Mouton Rothchild, or Chateau Hospice de Bon.

If your pocketbook is only so-so, an imported Bordeaux, such as St. Julien or a plain Margeaux will do nearly as well. If the state of your pocketbook dictates that you must descend to the domestic wines, don't feel too badly. These are improving all the time, and your local wine man can steer you to one that is more than acceptable.

I have mentioned before that the fat of duck is high proof and you really need a wine to break it down and handle it, once it gets inside you.

If you have either room or inclination for dessert, make it light—fresh fruit or a jelly.

After this meal, you will feel a discount of about twenty-five per cent on your age and all will seem right with an otherwise troubled world.

You can collapse into an easy chair and live over again, in digestive contemplation, the cold December morning, the rising sun, the decoys bobbing on the waves, and the approaching snarl of ducks, the flat, hollow sound of the guns, the good shots and the poor shots, the strenuous job of retrieving and, lastly, the warm and heartening companionship of it all.

It's a wonderful sport.

HUNTING RECORDS

Some gunners enjoy keeping a record of what they shoot, with whom they shoot, and the conditions under which the shooting is done. The following pages, blank except for headings, are placed in this book for their convenience.

It is the belief of the author that similar wind, barometric and temperature conditions on different days often bring about substantially similar shooting conditions.

If you are fortunate enough to have access to more than one blind site, a record of what happened at one blind site last year and the year before under certain weather conditions will help you to decide which blind to use this year on a day when the weather is about the same.

HUNTING CHART

DATE	NAMES OF COMPANIONS	LOCATION OF BLIND OR SHOOT	WEATHER			SHELLS EXPENDED	QUANTITIES AND/OR KINDS OF DUCKS OBSERVED	NUMBERS AND KINDS OF DUCKS TAKEN
			WIND	TEMPER-ATURE	BAROM-ETER			

HUNTING CHART

DATE	NAMES OF COMPANIONS	LOCATION OF BLIND OR SHOOT	WEATHER			SHELLS EXPENDED	QUANTITIES AND/OR KINDS OF DUCKS OBSERVED	NUMBERS AND KINDS OF DUCKS TAKEN
			WIND	TEMPER-ATURE	BAROM-ETER			

HUNTING CHART

DATE	NAMES OF COMPANIONS	LOCATION OF BLIND OR SHOOT	WEATHER			SHELLS EXPENDED	QUANTITIES AND/OR KINDS OF DUCKS OBSERVED	NUMBERS AND KINDS OF DUCKS TAKEN
			WIND	TEMPER-ATURE	BAROM-ETER			

HUNTING CHART

DATE	NAMES OF COMPANIONS	LOCATION OF BLIND OR SHOOT	WEATHER			SHELLS EXPENDED	QUANTITIES AND/OR KINDS OF DUCKS OBSERVED	NUMBERS AND KINDS OF DUCKS TAKEN
			WIND	TEMPER- ATURE	BAROM- ETER			

HUNTING CHART

DATE	NAMES OF COMPANIONS	LOCATION OF BLIND OR SHOOT	WEATHER			SHELLS EXPENDED	QUANTITIES AND/OR KINDS OF DUCKS OBSERVED	NUMBERS AND KINDS OF DUCKS TAKEN
			WIND	TEMPER-ATURE	BAROM-ETER			

HUNTING CHART

DATE	NAMES OF COMPANIONS	LOCATION OF BLIND OR SHOOT	WEATHER			SHELLS EXPENDED	QUANTITIES AND/OR KINDS OF DUCKS OBSERVED	NUMBERS AND KINDS OF DUCKS TAKEN
			WIND	TEMPER-ATURE	BAROM-ETER			

HUNTING CHART

DATE	NAMES OF COMPANIONS	LOCATION OF BLIND OR SHOOT	WEATHER			SHELLS EXPENDED	QUANTITIES AND/OR KINDS OF DUCKS OBSERVED	NUMBERS AND KINDS OF DUCKS TAKEN
			WIND	TEMPER-ATURE	BAROM-ETER			

HUNTING CHART

DATE	NAMES OF COMPANIONS	LOCATION OF BLIND OR SHOOT	WEATHER			SHELLS EXPENDED	QUANTITIES AND/OR KINDS OF DUCKS OBSERVED	NUMBERS AND KINDS OF DUCKS TAKEN
			WIND	TEMPER- ATURE	BAROM- ETER			

HUNTING CHART

DATE	NAMES OF COMPANIONS	LOCATION OF BLIND OR SHOOT	WEATHER			SHELLS EXPENDED	QUANTITIES AND/OR KINDS OF DUCKS OBSERVED	NUMBERS AND KINDS OF DUCKS TAKEN
			WIND	TEMPER-ATURE	BAROM-ETER			

HUNTING CHART

DATE	NAMES OF COMPANIONS	LOCATION OF BLIND OR SHOOT	WEATHER			SHELLS EXPENDED	QUANTITIES AND/OR KINDS OF DUCKS OBSERVED	NUMBERS AND KINDS OF DUCKS TAKEN
			WIND	TEMPER-ATURE	BAROM-ETER			

HUNTING CHART

DATE	NAMES OF COMPANIONS	LOCATION OF BLIND OR SHOOT	WEATHER			SHELLS EXPENDED	QUANTITIES AND/OR KINDS OF DUCKS OBSERVED	NUMBERS AND KINDS OF DUCKS TAKEN
			WIND	TEMPER-ATURE	BAROM-ETER			

HUNTING CHART

DATE	NAMES OF COMPANIONS	LOCATION OF BLIND OR SHOOT	WEATHER			SHELLS EXPENDED	QUANTITIES AND/OR KINDS OF DUCKS OBSERVED	NUMBERS AND KINDS OF DUCKS TAKEN
			WIND	TEMPER- ATURE	BAROM- ETER			

HUNTING CHART

DATE	NAMES OF COMPANIONS	LOCATION OF BLIND OR SHOOT	WEATHER			SHELLS EXPENDED	QUANTITIES AND/OR KINDS OF DUCKS OBSERVED	NUMBERS AND KINDS OF DUCKS TAKEN
			WIND	TEMPER- ATURE	BAROM- ETER			

HUNTING CHART

DATE	NAMES OF COMPANIONS	LOCATION OF BLIND OR SHOOT	WEATHER			SHELLS EXPENDED	QUANTITIES AND/OR KINDS OF DUCKS OBSERVED	NUMBERS AND KINDS OF DUCKS TAKEN
			WIND	TEMPER- ATURE	BAROM- ETER			

HUNTING CHART

DATE	NAMES OF COMPANIONS	LOCATION OF BLIND OR SHOOT	WEATHER			SHELLS EXPENDED	QUANTITIES AND/OR KINDS OF DUCKS OBSERVED	NUMBERS AND KINDS OF DUCKS TAKEN
			WIND	TEMPER- ATURE	BAROM- ETER			

UNTING CHART

DATE	NAMES OF COMPANIONS	LOCATION OF BLIND OR SHOOT	WEATHER			SHELLS EXPENDED	QUANTITIES AND/OR KINDS OF DUCKS OBSERVED	NUMBERS AND KINDS OF DUCKS TAKEN
			WIND	TEMPER-ATURE	BAROM-ETER			

INDEX